Lord Śiva's Song

While the Bhagavad Gītā is an acknowledged treasure of world spiritual literature, few people know a parallel text, the Īśvara Gītā. This lesser-known work is also dedicated to a god, but in this case it is Śiva, rather than Kṛṣṇa, who is depicted as the omniscient creator of the world. Andrew J. Nicholson's *Lord Śiva's Song* makes this text available in English in an accessible new translation. A work of poetry and philosophy, the Īśvara Gītā builds on the insights of Patañjali's Yoga Sūtra and foreshadows later developments in tantric yoga. It deals with the pluralistic religious environment of early medieval India through an exploration of the relationship between the gods Śiva and Viṣṇu. The work condemns sectarianism and violence, and provides a strategy for accommodating conflicting religious claims in its own day and in our own.

Andrew J. Nicholson is Associate Professor of Hinduism and Indian Intellectual History at the State University of New York, Stony Brook. His primary area of research is Indian philosophy and intellectual History, particularly medieval Vedanta and theistic yoga philosophies and their influence in the modern world. His first book, *Unifying Hinduism: Philosophy and Identity in Indian Intellectual History* and was awarded Best First Book in the History of Religions by the American Academy of Religion. This book is Professor Nicholson's second work and is an annotated translation of an eighth century Pāśupata Yoga text.

LORD ŚIVA'S SONG

The Īśvara Gītā

Translated with an Introduction and Notes by

Andrew J. Nicholson

MUNSHIRAM MANOHARLAL

Munshiram Manoharlal
Publishers Pvt. Ltd.

ISBN 978-81-215-1303-6
First Indian edition 2016

Printed in India
Published by Vikram Jain *for*
Munshiram Manoharlal Publishers Pvt. Ltd.
PO Box 5715, 54 Rani Jhansi Road, New Delhi 110 055, INDIA

www.mrmlbooks.com

To the memory of Shri Narayan Mishra

yasya deve parā bhaktir yathā deve tathā gurau

tasyaite kathitā hy arthāḥ prakāśante mahātmanaḥ

"These matters described by the great one

reveal themselves to the person

who shows the highest love toward god,

and as toward god, toward his own teacher."

—Śvetāśvatara Upaniṣad 6.23

Contents

Acknowledgments

The quest for liberation through yoga in medieval India, although sometimes depicted as a solitary endeavor, was more often a project involving an entire community of teachers and disciples. The same is true of the quest to complete a book such as this one. I have benefited enormously from the guidance and friendship of many scholars, only a few of whom I have the space to acknowledge here. First, I wish to offer thanks to my teachers in the United States and in India, especially to Shri Narayan Mishra, who helped me with this translation but passed away before publication.

I am very grateful to Stony Brook University, which granted me a semester research leave in 2009 to begin this project, and which also awarded me an FAHSS research grant to travel to Varanasi in 2011. Mario Piantelli was very kind to make his excellent Italian translation of the Īśvara Gītā available to me in digital form. The online text of the Kūrma Purāṇa and other Purāṇas provided by the Göttingen Register of Electronic Texts in Indian Languages (GRETIL) was also an important digital resource. My expert colleagues David Buchta, Whitney Cox, James Fitzgerald, Deven Patel, and Travis Smith read parts of my manuscript and offered invaluable advice. I presented parts of the introductory section of this book to audiences at the American Academy of Religion Annual Meeting in 2010, the Freie Universität Berlin Zukunftsphilologie Seminar in 2011, and the McGill University Faculty of Religious Studies Lecture Series in 2012. Their spirited, insightful questions have led me to refine my interpretations of the Īśvara Gītā and of Pāśupata philosophy. The students who read drafts of this work in undergraduate seminars with me at Stony Brook University offered suggestions to improve some of my unclear and ungainly translations. Finally, I thank my family, Claudia Misi, Silvia Nicholson, Marlene Nicholson, Norman Nicholson, and Elizabeth Nicholson, who have always sustained me with their love and encouragement.

Introduction

The Īśvara Gītā ("Lord Śiva's Song") is a philosophical poem that conveys the teachings of the Pāśupatas, a group of Śiva worshippers who would have a profound and lasting influence on the development of Hinduism. Since its composition in the eighth century CE, it has been an inspiration to generations of philosophers, devotees, and yogis in India. Like its famous predecessor, the Bhagavad Gītā ("Song of Lord Kṛṣṇa"), it goes beyond mere philosophical theory to describe a regimen of spiritual exercises to achieve self-transcendence and absolute freedom. These spiritual exercises, the "Pāśupata Yoga," are a regimen of ethical discipline, breath control, physical postures, and mental concentration through which the yogi attains divine knowledge, power, and liberation. Pāśupatas are not content just to know god. The ultimate goal of Pāśupata Yoga is to become god—to attain Lord Śiva's majestic power and wisdom in this very lifetime through mental absorption and union with him, the Lord of Yoga.

The proliferation of many different practices in the globalized yoga of the 20th and 21st centuries has led modern yogis to great uncertainty about what the final goal of yoga practice is: Is it stress relief? Peace of mind? Self-actualization? Nirvāṇa? Many teachers today describe Patañjali's Yoga Sūtras, an influential text compiled between the second and fifth centuries CE, as the authoritive set of guidelines for yoga practice. But examination of Patañjali's work reveals that many of the central ideas and practices of yoga as understood in later times are absent. One notable difference is Patañjali's relative lack of interest in physical postures (*āsanas*), the main focus of practice for many modern yogis. Another surprise for some Hindus might be the place of god (*īśvara*) in Patañjali's Yoga Sūtras. Although often described as the "classical Hindu" yoga, worship of and meditation on god is according to Patañjali a mere preliminary practice to the highest form of yoga.[1] This contrasts with the understanding of most Hindus, for whom god-absorption is the highest yogic practice.

The Īśvara Gītā, "Lord Śiva's Song," shows some influence from Patañjali's eight-limbed (*aṣṭāṅga*) yoga. According to this later text, however, Patañjali's highest form of mental absorption (*samādhi*) is a lower yoga, below absorption in god. The Īśvara Gītā also shares many concepts and themes with the famous Bhagavad Gītā, composed some six centuries earlier.[2] The most obvious difference between these two texts is the god who presents their teachings. In the Bhagavad Gītā, it is Kṛṣṇa, in disguise as a charioteer, who instructs the great warrior Arjuna on the subtleties of philosophy and sacred duty (*dharma*). In the Īśvara Gītā it is Śiva as Paśupati, Master of Beasts, who instructs a group of sages about the highest truth and the means to realize it through the practice of yoga. Śiva says that he himself is supreme, the source of creation for all other gods, and the ultimate focus of yogic concentration. In the popular imagination and especially among non-Hindus, Śiva is regarded as the god of destruction. However, according to the Pāśupatas who composed the Īśvara Gītā, he is something much more: the creator of the universe and the ultimate source of worldly bondage and liberation.

The Historical Background of the Īśvara Gītā

The earliest Hindu holy texts are the Vedas, composed in Sanskrit beginning in approximately 1500 BCE. For many Hindus, the Vedas are the absolute scriptural authority. According to traditional interpretation, the Vedas are eternal and beyond human authorship, received by ancient seers who spoke and memorized the words of the Vedas. Indeed, the word "scripture" is misleading insofar as the Vedas were oral texts not written down until hundreds of years after their composition. Scholars of the Vedas made a fundamental distinction between the eternal Vedas and other texts that were composed by human authors. In this second category are included the Bhagavad Gītā and Īśvara Gītā, both attributed to the sage Vyāsa. Although considered an omniscient seer, Vyāsa's texts and those composed by other great sages were not considered to have the same level of authority as the eternal Vedas. They were labeled "traditional" (*smṛti*) texts rather than the "revealed" (*śruti*) texts that make up the Vedas. The gods Śiva and Viṣṇu, prominently featured in Īśvara Gītā, are different than those emphasized in most of the Vedas. Yet an early form of Śiva is present in some form in the Vedas, known by another name, Rudra, "the roarer." Later parts of the Vedas, known as the Upaniṣads, show evidence of an increasing reverence for Rudra-Śiva. The Śvetāśvatara

Upaniṣad (circa third century BCE) describes Rudra as the supreme being and creator of the entire world. The themes of this monotheistic text went on to have a great influence on later religious literature, including the Bhagavad Gītā and Īśvara Gītā.[3]

The Purāṇas, a voluminous group of texts whose composition began around the fourth century CE, are the source of much of the mythology surrounding the god Śiva that has inspired Hindus in the medieval and modern periods. It is in the Purāṇas that we find the majority of texts known as Gītās, "songs." Like the Hindu epics the Mahābhārata and the Rāmāyana, the Purāṇas are "traditional," not "revealed." All these Purāṇas were regarded as the works of Vyāsa, an author of superhuman productivity, if we take these stories of authorship as historical fact. The Purāṇas are sometimes stereotyped as "mythological" texts. They certainly are a rich source of Hindu mythology, but they are also much more. Like the Mahābhārata, the Purāṇas are a vast repository of wisdom, containing sections on philosophy, theology, law, astrology, ritual theory, cosmology, and political science, usually combined in ways that defy tidy classification.[4] The Īśvara Gītā is itself a small section of one of these Purāṇas, the Kūrma Purāṇa ("Purāṇa of the Tortoise Incarnation").

The Purāṇas frequently present a trio of divine forms (the *trimūrti*), each form with a specific task: The god Brahmā is responsible for the world's creation, Viṣṇu for the world's preservation, and Śiva for the world's destruction. However, this formulation obscures the monotheistic orientation of many sections of the Purāṇas. The Īśvara Gītā teaches that although it may appear that Brahmā and Viṣṇu do their work independently from Śiva, the wise know that all the other gods are controlled by, and parts of, a single supreme deity. This single supreme deity is Lord Śiva.[5] Śiva is the one absolute god, and other gods mere aspects of the One. Like the Bhagavad Gītā and the Śvetāśvatara Upaniṣad, the Īśvara Gītā is not a polytheistic text, strictly speaking. Yet neither is it a monotheistic text in the same sense as the Bible or the Qur'an. In the monotheism of the Īśvara Gītā, the many gods are real and have real power in the world. But all their power is derived from the One, the supreme Śiva.

The Īśvara Gītā, although influential for medieval Hindus, was just one of the many sections labeled "Gītās" from the Purāṇas. Disregarded by most modern scholars of Hindu mythology for their philosophical focus, these Gītās also have been ignored by modern historians of Indian philosophy who do not usually think of the Purāṇas as quite properly philosophical. But premodern philosophers in India did not share this attitude toward the Purāṇas. The authors of the five Sanskrit commentaries on the Īśvara Gītā that have survived to the present day take this text every bit as seriously as the Bhagavad Gītā. One even suggests the Bhagavad Gītā and Īśvara Gītā are in essence the same teaching.[6] It makes sense that these Hindu philosophers would have treated the Īśvara Gītā, and the Purāṇas in general, with such reverence. If the sage Vyāsa composed the Mahābhārata and all of the many Purāṇas, then the Īśvara Gītā and the Bhagavad Gītā must present the same philosophy. How could an omniscient sage change his mind or contradict himself?

In the modern era, influential Hindu reformers such as Gandhi, Aurobindo, and Radhakrishnan have departed from premodern attitudes about the Vedas' authorship and the omniscience of the author(s) of the Purāṇas.[7] It is now widely accepted by Hindus and non-Hindus alike that the Purāṇas, the Mahābhārata, and the Rāmāyaṇa were each composed by more than one person over the course of several centuries, and that some of the thematic shifts we see within these texts are due to shifts in authorship.[8] Yet if the Mahābhārata and the Purāṇas were not all composed by a single author, and were instead composed over the course of many centuries, who were the true authors and compilers of these texts? How should we approach the Purāṇas' frequent repetitions of themes and stories found in the Mahābhārata, in particular? Are the Purāṇas muddled, superstitious texts, products of a later degenerate phase of Hinduism?

Intertextuality and Hinduism: The Īśvara Gītā, the Bhagavad Gītā, and the Yoga Sūtras

The Īśvara Gītā has been dismissed by some in the modern period because of its apparent borrowings from the Bhagavad Gītā. In the words of the 20th-century Sanskritist Franklin Edgerton, the Īśvara Gītā is an "imitative performance," "pale and lifeless" in comparison to its original.[9] Many Western Indologists and modern Hindu reformers shared this assessment of the Īśvara Gītā, and of the Purāṇas in general. One powerful example of modern anti-Purāṇic attitudes comes from Swami Dayananda Saraswati (1824–1883), founder of the influential Arya Samaj ("Society of Nobles") reform movement. Dayananda opposed idolatry in all its forms and saw the Vedas as preaching a rational worship of a formless and nameless ultimate God. Although some Hindus who believe in a God beyond forms might maintain that idol-worship is a "ladder" whereby the uneducated are able to approach the absolute reality, Dayananda emphatically disagreed. According to him:

> The method of worshipping through idols was introduced by the tantras and purāṇas. . . . Idol-worship is not a ladder. It is a big ditch, by falling into which man is smashed to pieces. He can never come out of it and is sure to remain there till he dies. . . . Nobody has ever become learned by the worship of idols. All idolators remain ignorant till death overcomes them and terminates their unsuccessful career.[10]

Dayananda maintained that the Purāṇas were the not true works of Vyāsa, but rather works of later authors "in the name of Vyāsa . . . full of ridiculous and credulous stories."[11] Although contemporary scholars would agree with Dayananda's assessment that the Purāṇas were not all composed by a single author, many would argue that Dayananda sells the Purāṇas short. Besides providing immense amounts of data for historians who wish to understand the development of medieval Hinduism, the Purāṇas are also a vast repository of wisdom, a continuation of the insights of the Vedas and epics.[12]

The Bhagavad Gītā, a section of the epic Mahābhārata, has been considered by Gandhi and many other modern Hindus as the closest equivalent that Hinduism has to a Bible. Its fame has been so overpowering that many Hindus themselves are unaware that it is only one among dozens of texts in Sanskrit known as "Gītās" or "songs."[13] These Gītās are philosophical dialogues written in verse, and often involve a conversation between an omniscient deity and one or more human beings. The themes of these other Gītās often overlap with the Bhagavad Gītā, especially in their focus on *bhakti* (devotion to god) and on the practice of yoga. But they were written after the Bhagavad Gītā, often by many centuries, and their teachings mark further elaborations of the themes found in earlier texts. Some medieval Gītās present teachings of tantric yoga, including such now-familiar ideas as cosmic union of male and female principles represented by the ascent of the *kuṇḍalinī* serpent through the subtle energy centers known as *cakras*.[14] The Īśvara Gītā stands at an important transitional stage before the widespread influence of tantra but after the "classical" yoga of Patañjali. It shows the unmistakable influence of Patañjali's Yoga Sūtras in its elaboration of the eightfold (*aṣṭāṅga*) yoga, yet it goes beyond him. In chapter 11, the Īśvara Gītā teaches that the "aloneness" (*kaivalya*) presented by Patañjali as the highest goal is only a preliminary step on the way to the highest yoga, the union of the individual self with Lord Śiva.

Instead of criticizing the Īśvara Gītā and other works in Sanskrit that copy pieces of earlier texts as mere imitations, we should try the imaginative exercise of putting ourselves in the situation of the audiences for these "imitative" texts. The readers or listeners of the Īśvara Gītā certainly were not fooled into thinking that the copied verses were new and original to the Īśvara Gītā. On the contrary, the quotations from the Bhagavad Gītā in this text were designed to be noticed. Instead of weakening the authority of the Īśvara Gītā, such borrowing strengthens it. In the Sanskrit textual traditions of which the Īśvara Gītā is a part, novelty is not a virtue; it is a defect. The Īśvara Gītā, the Bhagavad Gītā, and other "traditional" (*smṛti*) texts insist that they are not presenting new teachings. They say that in fact, all they are doing is re-presenting in a new format the teachings of the revealed (*śruti*) texts that came before them, the Vedas. Likewise, medieval commentators on the Īśvara Gītā and the Bhagavad Gītā insist that they are simply uncovering meanings that are already present in those texts, not innovating or adding any new meanings of their own. In this literary universe so different from ours today, for innovation to be accepted, it had to wear the cloak of tradition.

Just as its is possible to treat the Purāṇas as appendices to the Mahābhārata, picking up and expanding on many of the stories and ideas therein, so too the Īśvara Gītā often expands on the Bhagavad Gītā, picking up philosophical ideas that were merely hinted at in the Bhagavad Gītā and putting them at the forefront of the later text. One marked example of this is the concept of *māyā* ("magical power"), which makes a fleeting appearance in the Bhagavad Gītā.[15] In the Īśvara Gītā the idea of magical power, the power that god employs to conceal the true nature of things from worldly creatures, becomes a major theme. The word *māyā* is used thirty-two times. The Īśvara Gītā also describes god as the *māyin*, magician, who creates forms in the world by means of his magical power, a feminine force. A related theme is the use of the imagery of human sexual procreation as a metaphor for god's creative process in the world. The idea that the ultimate god contains both masculine and feminine aspects is a familiar one from later Hindu theology, such as Rāmānuja's Śrī Vaiṣṇava school. Verses 14.3–4 of the Bhagavad Gītā teach,

> My womb is the great infinite spirit;
> in it I place the embryo,
> and from this, Arjuna,
> comes the origin of all creatures.
>
> The infinite spirit is the great womb
> of all forms that come to be
> In all wombs,
> and I am the seed-giving father.[16]

The authors of the Īśvara Gītā eagerly expand this metaphor, showing even more explicitly how the ultimate god Śiva is an androgyne, containing both masculine and feminine characteristics:

> Great *brahman* is my womb.
> That is where I place the seed.
> It is the source named magical power,
> and from it the entire world is born . . .
>
> Magical power is the supreme womb
> of the forms that are born
> in the wombs of all beings.
> Sages know that I am the father.
>
> The wise one who recognizes me
> as inseminator, father, and ruler
> does not become deluded
> in any of the worlds.[17]

Action and Renunciation

Despite the obvious thematic similarities between the Bhagavad Gītā and Īśvara Gīta, there are important differences in tone and emphasis. The Bhagavad Gītā is primarily a text for householders, those members of society like the warrior Arjuna who are engaged in worldly pursuits: marrying, having children, making a living, and (in Arjuna's case) fighting battles. Its continuing relevance, especially in the minds of modern Hindu thinkers like Gandhi and Tilak, was in its teaching of *karma-yoga*, the yoga of action.[18] Must one renounce career and family to achieve the highest goal of life, liberation from the cycle of death and rebirth? According to ancient Indian theories of action (*karma*), any worldly pursuit involves the accumulation of karmic fruits, and these karmic fruits ensure continuous rebirth from lifetime to lifetime. Even the priest performing the sacrifices enjoined by the Vedas ties himself down to the world through his sacrificial action. The fruits of his actions may be positive, ensuring future rebirths in bodies rewarded with comfort and worldly success. Nonetheless, such actions lead the individual no closer to the ultimate goal of freedom from rebirth in the cycle of *saṃsāra*. Following this line of thinking, only by abandoning all action, both meritorious and demeritorious, and becoming a renouncer (*saṃnyāsin*) can one hope to achieve liberation at some future time.[19]

The Bhagavad Gītā's teaching of action without concern for the fruits of action presented a solution to the householder's conundrum.

Beginning in its second chapter, the god Kṛṣṇa teaches that it is possible for someone like Arjuna to pursue his caste responsibilities and still be liberated. Instead of throwing down his bow and renouncing all action, Arjuna must become a renouncer internally. By following his duties without any concern for the positive karmic results that will accrue, it is possible for Arjuna, and for all people regardless of class (*varṇa*) and stage of life (*āśrama*), to achieve liberation while engaged in a life of action. Reinterpreted not primarily as a call to perform traditional duties but rather as a call to progressive social activism, this message inspired Gandhi and his followers to fight for the rights of widows and untouchables, breaking away from earlier attitudes about ritual purity and pollution.[20]

From its very first chapter, it is clear that the Īśvara Gītā's social milieu is quite different. Instead of focusing on the responsibilities of the householder to act, the Īśvara Gītā teaches that renunciation accompanied by yoga is the highest way to know god. Borrowing from the Yoga Sūtra of Patañjali, another renouncer text, the Īśvara Gītā demands celibacy (*brahmacārya*) and nonacquisition (*aparigraha*) as preparatory steps to higher levels of yogic perfection.[21] Śiva's teaching in this text is not primarily directed toward a warrior (*kṣatriya*) like Arjuna who struggles with this-worldly moral dilemmas. Rather, it is for the Brahmin renouncers who have gathered at a remote, sacred site in the Himālayas to try to clarify their confusion. This confusion is not about their worldly duties in society, but rather about metaphysics: "Who is the lord who causes others to be reborn? Who sees everything? What is the highest *brahman*?"[22] Although the Bhagavad Gītā eventually gets around to answering these questions, it begins with a this-worldly inquiry on the nature of duty and sacrifice. The first chapter of the Īśvara Gītā dives immediately into the deep end of Hindu metaphysics and cosmology, and at first glance may seem less approachable for the modern reader than the Bhagavad Gītā.

On the other hand, the Īśvara Gītā's advantage over the Bhagavad Gītā is that it goes into much greater detail about the practice of yoga. In a few famous verses the Bhagavad Gītā sketches how and where a yogi should practice, but its primary concern is the householder's success in fulfilling his worldly duties with the right mental attitude.[23] As a meditation manual, it leaves a great deal out. What is breath control (*prāṇayāma*), and what are its effects? What types of mantras should one recite? Most importantly, how can the yogi cultivate the meditative concentration (*dhyāna*) that leads to liberation? Chapter 11 of the Īśvara Gītā systematically details the eight limbs of yoga, including discussions of specific postures, moral observations, breath control exercises, and vividly described visualization techniques. The ground covered by the chapter will be familiar to readers of Patañjali's Yoga Sūtra, as the eight limbs (*aṅgas*) of yoga are the same in both texts. But Patañjali leaves out what the Īśvara Gītā considers most important of all. For the yogi to be truly liberated, he must first become god.

Philosophy and Practice: The Pāśupata Path of Godhood

Śaivas, those Hindus who take Śiva as the single highest god, were a powerful force in medieval South and Southeast Asia, but the history of their origins is still cloaked in mystery. The Pāśupatas, the earliest recorded group of Śaivas, are mentioned in the Mahābhārata, the famous Hindu epic poem.[24] These ascetics took the name "Pāśupata" from the form of Śiva they worshipped, Paśupati, "The Master of Beasts." The Pāśupatas occupied an ambiguous place among Hindu traditions. Although today they are understood as a seminal influence on later Hinduism, in their time they often were criticized and considered beyond the pale of the Vedic mainstream, especially in the eyes of the orthoprax Brahmins who concerned themselves with the preservation of the Vedas and the correct performance of Vedic rituals.[25] This liminal position is reflected in the Purāṇas, where the Pāśupatas are at turns celebrated and reviled, sometimes in the very same text.

The defenders of the Vedas often may have seen the Pāśupatas as a threat, but the Pāśupatas were conscious of their connection to Vedic tradition, presenting themselves as its true heirs. Central to the liturgy of the Pāśupatas was the Śatarudrīya, "Hymn to the Thousand forms of Rudra," which appears in the Yajur Veda.[26] Unlike later tantric worshippers of Śiva, they also adhered to many of the social attitudes of Vedic religion by drawing distinctions between the four classes (*varṇas*). According to the tradition of the Pāśupata Sūtras, initiation is only available to Brahmin males, and the Pāśupata yogi should never even speak with low castes or women.[27] One name associated with the Pāśupata sect, "the way beyond" (*atimarga*), expresses the idea that the adept has passed beyond the four stages of life outlined in the Hindu legal texts, and is on a path more rarified and demanding than the path of the orthoprax renouncer (*saṃnyāsin*) described in mainstream texts.[28] Like later Śaivas, the Pāśupata imitates Śiva by taking on his outward appearance (matted hair, skin smeared with ash) and antisocial behavior (gesticulating wildly, making loud noises and lewd gestures). At a higher and more meaningful level, this means becoming Śiva by taking on his lordly powers. Through meditative contact with Śiva, the Pāśupata yogi receives his powers, like a flame passed from candle to candle.

The Pāśupatas, like some of the later groups they influenced, introduce three ontological categories to explain the state of suffering experienced by most beings. The first category is *pati,* "master," Lord Śiva himself. Śiva is the cause and creator of all beings. He is their protector, and it is he who is ultimately responsible for bondage and liberation. The *paśu,* or "beast," refers to an individual self (*jīvātman*) who is bound to the cycle of death and rebirth, not yet liberated. Finally, the third category is the *pāśa,* "fetter." It is through the fetters created by god that selves are bound to the cycle of suffering and rebirth. Yet it is also through the master that such beasts have their fetters removed. The wise know it is ultimately Lord Śiva's grace (*prasāda*), and not the individual efforts of the yogi, that allows the individual to join the ranks of the *siddhas,* liberated beings who have permanently become free from suffering by means of Pāśupata yoga.[29] The playful image invoked through this trio of alliterative words—*pati, paśu, pāśa*—is, of course, the nomadic life of the pastoral cattle-herder. Śiva protects his herd of beasts (*paśus*) even as he keeps them in fetters (*pāśas*). But why does Śiva do any of this at all? What is the point of Śiva's elaborate game in which some selves are bound in chains even as others are freed? Chapter seven of the Īśvara Gītā suggests that this is all part of god's play (*līlā*):

> All selves that undergo the cycle
> of rebirth are called "beasts."
> I am god, their master. The wise
> know me as the "master of beasts."
>
> In my play, I ensnare those beasts
> using the fetters of magical power.
> Those who speak of the Veda call me
> the one who frees the beasts.
>
> There is no liberator of those
> ensnared in the fetters of magical power
> other than me, the highest self,
> the immortal ruler of beings.[30]

The Pāśupata Sūtras and their commentaries teach that the yogic adept (*sādhaka*) undertakes a vow that consists of three stages. In the first, the Pāśupata should live at or near a Śaiva temple, should bear the mark of the Pāśupata ascetic by bathing in ash, and worship Śiva with song, dance, laughter, and mantra repetition.[31] The initiate also adopts a set of moral precepts similar to those outlined in Patañjali's Yoga Sūtras, including non-harming (*ahiṃsā*), celibacy (*brahmacārya*), and truthfulness (*satya*).[32] The idea of yogis singing and dancing defies the common stereotype of yogis as solitary, stationary, and solely concerned with inward contemplation. Furthermore, these were not mere spontaneous gestures of devotion or simple oral folk traditions. Kauṇḍinya says that the singing of the Pāśupata yogi should be "in accord with the Gandharva Śāstra" and his dancing "in accord with the Nāṭya Śāstra," presumably meaning the classic work composed by Bharata.[33] Although these passages may force us to adjust our ideas of what is proper behavior for a yogi, on second thought it should be hardly surprising that medieval yogis would include training in dance as part of the path to union with Śiva. Śiva is famous as Nāṭarāja, "Lord of the Dance." It is this form that is portrayed in the climactic fifth chapter of the Īśvara Gītā, when Śiva displays his wondrous dance in the sky above the Badarikā hermitage where the yogis are assembled.

The second of the three stages of the Pāśupata vow has attracted more attention than almost all other aspects of the Pāśupata path, as it involves transgressions of the normal conventions of society, reminiscent in some ways of the practice of shamelessness among the Cynics of ancient Greece.[34] During this stage he discards the mark (*liṅga*) of the Pāśupata ascetic, and enters the public square snoring, trembling, limping, making obscene gestures to young women, and babbling as if drunk or insane.[35] His goal in this practice is to purify himself by receiving the abuse of others. All these behaviors are an act, as he has not given up his previous vows of celibacy (*brahmacarya*) and mindfulness (*apramāda*). Instead, he engages in a different kind of spiritual exercise, one practiced only rarely by Śaiva ascetics today. Because one of the most powerful human motivations is to receive praise and avoid blame, by learning to "despise praise like a poison" and take pleasure in insult, the Pāśupata adept cuts off yet another tie that binds Hindus who remain in the first four stages of life.[36] These practices earned the Pāśupatas notoriety among other sects and philosophical traditions. In modern works on Indian philosophy and religion they are still mentioned more often for this than for their strict ethical precepts or theology of union with Śiva. In the third and final stage of the Pāśupata vow, the adept withdraws from society and moves into a vacant house or cave.[37] Then, after six months of uninterrupted meditation on the syllable Oṃ and union with Śiva, he moves to a cremation ground.[38] There he achieves complete union with Śiva, cutting off karma at its root. By the grace of Śiva, he achieves the end of suffering and eternal freedom.[39]

Mainstreaming Pāśupata Practice

Although in verse 11.67 the Īśvara Gītā describes its teachings as "Pāśupata Yoga," many statements of the Īśvara Gītā appear to contradict the teachings of the Pāśupata Sūtras (circa second century CE) and its commentary by Kauṇḍinya (circa fourth to sixth centuries CE). So, for instance, the Īśvara Gītā follows the Bhagavad Gītā in portraying Sāṃkhya and Yoga teachings in a positive light. In chapter 11, the Īśvara Gītā presents the eight limbs of yoga in a way nearly identical to Patañjali's Yoga Sūtras, not mentioning important differences in the lists of restraints (*yamas*) and observances (*niyamas*) between Patañjali's Yoga and Pāśupata Yoga. By contrast, Kauṇḍinya's commentary on the Pāśupata Sūtras repeatedly rejects and criticizes Patañjali's Yoga, describing it as "devoid of right knowledge" and describing the followers of Patañjali as "beasts" (*paśus*) who have not yet escaped from their bondage in the cycle of death and rebirth.[40]

Another feature of the Īśvara Gītā that may be confusing is its frequent use of concepts familiar from Vedānta. In particular, the important Vedāntic terms *ātman* ("self") and *brahman* ("ultimate reality") appear frequently. The Vedānta school of philosophy based itself on the systematic interpretation of the Upaniṣads, and the exploration of the relation between self and ultimate reality detailed there. But there is great variation in the interpretations of the different subschools of Vedānta, despite their common focus. The most well-known subschool of Vedānta in the modern period, Śaṅkara's Advaita (nondualist) Vedānta, taught that in ultimate truth *brahman* is beyond the gods, and completely without qualities (*nirguṇa*). Although devotion to god might have some limited benefits, according to Śaṅkara only knowledge of the highest *brahman* without qualities leads to liberation.[41] However, other Vedāntins such as Rāmānuja and Śrīkaṇṭha were theists who taught that references to *brahman* in the Upaniṣads were references to an all-powerful personal god. According to Rāmānuja, that ultimate god is Viṣṇu, whereas Śrīkaṇṭha, a Śaiva, argued that Śiva is highest. Both the Īśvara Gītā and Bhagavad Gītā are generally more amenable to a theistic interpretation than to Śaṅkara's non-theistic position, although Śaṅkara did in fact write a commentary on the Bhagavad Gītā.[42] Some other concepts found in the Īśvara Gītā, such as the notion of the world as god's play (*līlā*), are not found in the Pāśupata Sūtras but are similar to later theistic Vedānta.[43]

A very important issue taken up by the Pāśupata Sūtras is the question of who has the qualification (*adhikāra*) to practice Pāśupata yoga. Although Kauṇḍinya understands only Brahmins to be qualified, there is no stipulation in the Īśvara Gītā that the highest yoga is only open to Brahmins, nor is there any echo of the Pāśupata Sūtras' prohibition from interacting with people of the servant class (*śūdras*) and women.[44] Kauṇḍinya is aware that in the course of begging for alms, the Pāśupata mendicant will see and may even have to talk to *śūdras* and women. He therefore prescribes a purificatory ritual of bathing in ashes and breath exercises (*prāṇayāma*) that the Pāśupata yogi should practice whenever he sees urine, feces, a *śūdra*, or a woman. We can see from this that in spite of its influence on what would eventually become tantric Saivism, the Pāśupatas who followed Kauṇḍinya had drastically different attitudes to purity and pollution than did later tantric yogis. Kauṇḍinya's commentary is also notoriously misogynistic. In his discussion of celibacy, he describes women as "poison," and "the root of all evils."[45]

The Īśvara Gītā, however, shows no such hostility toward *śūdras* and women. Although it tends to focus on the life of Brahmin male, as do most texts of its time period, it does not agree with Kauṇḍinya that only Brahmin men can achieve liberation through union with Lord Śiva. Here the Īśvara Gītā instead follows the Bhagavad Gītā's lead in suggesting that by the grace of god, union with Śiva is also a possibility for the low born.[46] In chapter 4 of the Īśvara Gītā, Lord Śiva says:

> Virtuous brahmins, warriors,
> and merchants worship me.
> I grant them the state of bliss,
> the supreme abode.
>
> Even servants and others of low birth
> who pursue forbidden occupations
> are in time freed and joined to me
> if they are full of devotion.[47]

How can we account for the differences between the Īśvara Gītā's portrayal of Pāśupata Yoga and the portrayal in the Pāśupata Sūtras? One intriguing possibility is that the Īśvara Gītā expressed a kind of "exoteric" or "mainstream" form of Pāśupatism.[48] Although the Īśvara Gītā repeats again and again the idea that its ideas are secret and should only be shared with a select few, in practice this was not the case. In contrast to the Pāśupata Sūtras, the Īśvara Gītā was a part of the popular Kūrma Purāṇa, and as a result would have had a wide readership of many different types of Hindus, not only Śiva worshippers. If the Īśvara Gītā was indeed a later insertion into the Kūrma Purāṇa, a text originally affiliated with Vaiṣṇavaism, the Īśvara Gītā may have been one of several attempts throughout the Purāṇas to "mainstream" Pāśupatism by portraying it in a sympathetic and relatively sectarian-neutral light. This also would account for the frequency of Vedāntic, Sāṃkhya, and Pātañjala themes in the Īśvara Gītā less common in the Pāśupata Sūtras and their commentaries.

However, it is also clear that not all of the authors of various sections of the Kūrma Purāṇa had a positive attitude toward the Pāśupatas. Looking at the different parts that make up the Kūrma Purāṇa, the Pāśupatas are more often celebrated than criticized. Some of the criticisms in the text, however, are severe. For instance, in the section that comes directly after the Īśvara Gītā, a treatise on the *dharma* of the householder called the "Song of Vyāsa" (Vyāsa Gītā), the sage Vyāsa reviles Pāśupatas and two other sects:

> Do not interact, even just in speech,
> with the heretics who engage in wrong action:
> Tantrics of the left-hand,
> Pañcarātras, and Pāśupatas.[49]

Elsewhere in the Vyāsa Gītā, Pāśupatas are classified as heretics (*pāṣaṇḍas*) alongside Buddhists, Jains, Pañcarātras, and Kāpālikas. In that section, Vyāsa warns that anyone who consorts with such people will not be able to successfully perform the ancestral (*śrāddha*) rites.[50] It is clear that the Pāśupata sect suffered from an image problem in early medieval India. This problem was especially actute among *smarta* Brahmin householders concerned with upholding the ritual order of their forefathers, which had come under attack by the Buddhist, Jain, and Hindu renouncers. It is therefore especially notable that the Īśvara Gītā moderates the Pāśupatas' hard-line stance against the ritual sacrifice of animals. Like Patañjali's Yoga Sūtras, the Pāśupata Sūtras maintained a strict adherence to non-harming (*ahiṃsā*) in all situations, even when the Vedas explicitly demand performance of animal sacrifice. For Vedic traditions, this was among the most threatening of the yogis' teachings.[51] However, the Īśvara Gītā contains a subtle and important re-definition of the concept of non-harming (*ahiṃsā*):

> The great sages define non-harming
> as not causing pain to any living

being anywhere, whether through
physical action, thoughts, or speech.

There is no *dharma* higher than non-harming.
It is the greatest happiness. But harming
when following scripture's injunction
should be considered non-harming.[52]

This conciliatory attitude, mostly absent in the Pāśupata Sūtras and Patañjali's Yoga Sūtras, shows willingness to compromise on questions that many yogis would have considered non-negotiable.[53] This proviso in the Īśvara Gītā may well have been inspired by a famous verse from the Laws of Manu, where Manu teaches that "when *hiṃsā* is sanctioned by the Veda and well established in this mobile and immobile creation, it should be regarded definitely as *ahiṃsā*; for it is from the Veda that the Law has shined forth."[54] Although everyday acts of violence, such as hunting animals for a meal, would still have violated this revised understanding of the teaching of non-harming, it allowed Vedic ritualists to continue to pursue their animal sacrifices without the taint of demerit. This concern for rapprochement between Pāśupata Yoga and Vedic sacrificial traditions, largely absent from Kauṇḍinya's commentary on the Pāśupata Sūtras, is a remarkable feature of the exoteric Pāśupata teachings of the Īśvara Gītā.

The Yoga of the Pāśupatas

At the beginning of chapter 11 of the Īśvara Gītā, Lord Śiva presents two different kinds of yoga, one called "the yoga of non-being" (*abhāva-yoga*), the other "the great yoga" (*mahā-yoga*):

Those who are yoked to this yoga on me,
whether once daily, twice daily,
three times daily, or all the time,
should be known as the "great lords."

But yoga is known to be of two kinds.
The first is considered the yoga
of non-being. The other is the
great yoga, the very best of all yogas.

The yoga in which one's own essence
is known to be empty, free from all

false appearances, is named the yoga
of non-being. Through it, one sees the self.

The yoga in which one discerns the self
as eternally blissful, free from blemish,
and united with me is called
the great yoga of the supreme lord.[55]

Despite the use of the word "empty" (*śūnya*), the "yoga of non-being" described here is not Buddhist yoga.[56] Rather, it refers to cessative yogas such as Patañjali's that do not understand the ultimate state of liberation as union with a supreme deity or ultimate reality. By means of the cessation (*nirodha*) of mental activity, such yogas enable the practitioner to discern the existence of a pure, eternal self free from the world of matter (*prakṛti*). This yoga of non-being does not, however, reveal the self's unity with Lord Śiva. It is useful as a means to discriminate between the true, eternal self and the egoistic self that is subject to change, a preparatory practice for liberation. But it is powerless to move the yogi from this dualistic discernment of the self's ontological difference from material nature to the higher knowledge of the self's oneness with God.[57]

This distinction between the two yogas is reminiscent of another Pāśupata text, Kauṇḍinya's commentary on the Pāśupata Sūtras. There too, the Sāṃkhya-influenced Yoga philosophy of Patañjali is mentioned and given lower status than the yoga of the Pāśupatas. But the way the Īśvara Gītā and Kauṇḍinya's commentary on the Pāśupata Sūtras present issues of ritual and doctrinal diversity is different. The Īśvara Gītā emphasizes the preliminary value of the yoga of non-being, the cessative approach to yoga. By contrast, Kauṇḍinya repeatedly belittles followers of Patañjali. He writes, "those who have won [supposed] release through Sāṃkhya-Yoga, indeed all creatures from Brahmā down to the animals, are considered 'beasts.' "[58] Here Kauṇḍinya uses the word *paśu*, "beast," in its technical sense, referring to any self in bondage who has yet to be liberated. Although followers of Patañjali argue otherwise, they cannot truly be liberated unless they recognize their fundamental unity with God. Hence, Kauṇḍinya calls them "beasts." The Īśvara Gītā, however, does not dwell on this deficiency, simply presenting the yoga of non-being as a preparatory practice to the great yoga, the yoga of the Pāśupatas.

After chapter 11 introduces the distinction between the two yogas, it subsequently presents a fusion of Pāśupata and Pātañjala Yoga traditions. The most obvious borrowing from Patañjali is the text's adoption of his "eight limbs" (*aṣṭāṅga*) of Yoga. The Pāśupata Sūtras in fact have a different way of enumerating the path of yoga, which includes five categories (*arthas*), ten abstentions (*yamas*), and ten observances (*niyamas*).[59] This contrasts with the five abstentions and five observances presented in the Yoga Sūtras. Īśvara Gītā verses 11.11 to 11.45 present a fairly straightforward summary of Patañjali's eight limbs. Yet at this section's beginning, in its definition of the word *yoga*, it both alludes to and rejects Patañjali's understanding of yoga as "cessation of mental activity" (*citta-vṛtti-nirodha*). Here is how Lord Śiva begins his account of the eight limbs in the Īśvara Gītā:

> Breath control, meditation,
> sense withdrawal, concentration,
> absorption, abstentions, observances,
> and posture—Best of sages,
>
> *yoga* is the one-pointed focus
> of the mind on me through suppression
> of other mental activity.
> I have just told you its eight means.[60]

After enumerating the eight limbs of yoga, Lord Śiva here gives a definition of yoga that is both an allusion to and a departure from Patañjali's famous sūtra 1.2: "Yoga is the suppression of mental activity" (*yogaś citta-vṛtti-nirodhaḥ*). According to the Īśvara Gītā, the cessation of mental activity described by Patañjali is incomplete by itself, a mere means to the highest absorption in the Lord. This is accomplished by one-pointed mental focus (*eka-cittatā*) on Lord Śiva. Of course, meditation on the Lord does have some role to play in Patañjali's yoga as well: Called *īśvara-praṇidhāna*, it is classified as one of the five observances, or *niyamas*, in his scheme. As such is it is one of the preliminary practices that eventually lead to the higher forms of meditation and eventually to the transcendent state of aloneness (*kaivalya*). But for the Īśvara Gītā, mental focus on Lord Śiva is the highest yoga, whereas the Pātañjala Yoga's highest *samādhi* occupies a lower rung in the hierarchy of yogas.

Another piece of evidence suggesting that the Īśvara Gītā sought to present the Pāśupata Yoga in a positive light, minus any doctrines or practice that may have alienated the Purāṇas' wider audience, is the lack of mention of the practices of the second stage of the Pāśupata vow. Feigning madness in public and making lewd gestures were not standard practices for most renouncers in premodern India, and would have been difficult to explain to an audience without any particular knowledge of or allegiance to Pāśupatism. This second stage, and the rationale behind it, goes entirely unmentioned in the Īśvara Gītā. Instead the yoga path described hews closely to the eightfold path of Patañjali, but with a new Śiva-centric attitude. Although Patañjali lists "meditation on the lord" (*īśvara-praṇidhāna*) among the five observances (*niyamas*), the precise identity of the lord, and the precise meaning of the word *praṇidhāna*, have been open to multiple interpretations. It may even be argued that Patañjali was purposefully vague, refusing to identify "the lord" explicitly with Viṣṇu or Śiva, in order to avoid alienating any of his potential audience.[61] By contrast, the Īśvara Gītā is quite clear in its identification of Śiva as the lord. Instead of using Patañjali's ambiguous word *praṇidhāna* to describe this observance, it uses the term *īśvara-pūjana*, worship of Lord Śiva.

Above all, the special mark of Pāśupata practice was the smearing of ashes on the body. Although it is not discussed at length in the Īśvara Gītā, this remarkable practice is at least mentioned. It comes at the end of the description of a series of visualization exercises performed by the Pāśupata Yogi. These are what the Īśvara Gītā describes as the "great yoga" (*mahā-yoga*). It is the type of yoga that goes beyond the preparatory practice of "the yoga of non-being" (*abhāva-yoga*) exemplified by Patañjali and other yogis who present cessation (*nirodha*) of mental activity as the ultimate form of yoga. The exercises of the "great yoga" facilitate the yogi's identification with Lord Śiva until union (*saṃyoga*) is achieved:

> Binding himself in the *svastika*,
> lotus, or half posture, his gaze
> resting evenly on the tip of his nose,
> with eyes slightly open,
>
> calm and free from fear, he renounces
> this world consisting of magical power.
> He concentrates on the supreme lord,
> the god who resides in his own self.
>
> He then visualizes a lotus twelve
> fingers long on the tip of his topknot.
> It is beautiful, blooming from the bulb
> that is *dharma*. Its stalk is knowledge,
>
> the lordly powers its eight petals.
> It is completely white. Renunciation
> is its seed-cup. In that seed-cup he should
> visualize a sublime golden treasure.

Consisting of all of the powers,
directly they call it Oṃ, the divine,
eternal syllable, the unmanifest,
surrounded by a network of rays.

There he should think of
a pure, supreme, eternal light.
In that light he places his own self,
which is identical to it.

He meditates on the lord, highest cause,
standing in the middle of space.
At last, becoming the all-pervading
lord himself, he visualizes nothing.[62]

This practice is not just a mental exercise by which the yogi visualizes himself "as if" he were Lord Śiva. Rather, it is a transformative practice through which the yogi becomes the Lord. Throughout the Īśvara Gītā, accomplished yogis are called "Lords" (*īśvaras*), "Great Lords," (*maheśvaras*) or "Lords of Yoga" (*yogeśvaras*). It is sometimes unclear when the word "lord" (*īśvara*) is used if it is Lord Śiva or one of his Pāśupata followers who is meant. This ambiguity serves a purpose. It reinforces the central metaphysical assertion of the Pāśupata philosophy: At the highest level of yogic absorption, the difference between the meditating subject and the object of his meditation dissolves. The Īśvara Gītā's "one-pointed mental focus" on Śiva is ultimately the same as the "union of the individual self with the Lord" (*ātmeśvara-saṃyoga*) described in Kauṇḍinya's commentary on the Pāśupata Sūtras.

After detailing three visualization exercises, the Īśvara Gītā proclaims, "This Pāśupata yoga is for the liberation of creatures from their fetters. The Vedas declare it the essence of all the Upaniṣads, transcending the stages of life."[63] At this point, it is as if the authors of the Īśvara Gītā realize that they have gone too far, revealed too much, departed too drastically from the paradigm of the Bhagavad Gītā. For following this is a series of verses that borrow themes from the Bhagavad Gītā, in some cases in word-for-word imitation. These fifteen verses focus primarily on two themes: devotion to god (*bhakti*) and abandonment of the fruits of actions (*phala-tyāga*). Although the theme of devotion recurs throughout the Īśvara Gītā (and, of course, is a major theme of virtually all the Purāṇas), the theme of abandonment of fruits is relatively uncommon in the Īśvara Gītā. This is one of the major differences between the Īśvara Gītā and Bhagavad Gītā.

The authors of the Bhagavad Gītā redefined the meaning of renunciation to make sense in Arjuna's warrior milieu: Renunciation means renunciation of fruits, not renunciation of actions themselves. However, the Īśvara Gītā is ambiguous about which type of renunciation is preferable. Often, it preaches renunciation of all worldly activities, echoing Patañjali's teaching of celibacy (*brahmacarya*), austerity (*tapas*), and non-acquisition (*aparigraha*) in the first two limbs (*aṅgas*) of the Yoga Sūtra's eight-limbed yoga.

Unity and Diversity Among the Gods

As in the Bhagavad Gītā, another central concern of the Īśvara Gītā is to establish the ultimate unity of the gods. The Īśvara Gītā is primarily concerned with two: Śiva and Nārāyaṇa (also known as Viṣṇu). Nārāyaṇa, present from the very first chapter of the Īśvara Gītā, gives a kind of warm-up act before Śiva appears and begins his discourse to the sages. After Śiva's arrival, Nārāyaṇa sits beside Śiva admiringly and listens to his teaching. Near the end of the Īśvara Gītā's final chapter, Śiva finally explains that he and Nārāyaṇa are one. There is no possibility of liberation for those who shun his divine friend:

> Those people go to terrible hells
> who see me otherwise,
> thinking that he and I are different gods.
> I do not abide in them.
>
> I liberate those who take refuge in me:
> the fool and the scholar,
> the Brahmin and the dog-cooker,
> but not one who reviles Nārāyaṇa.
>
> Therefore, to give me pleasure,
> my devotees should
> praise him and bow to him,
> the highest spirit, the great yogi.[64]

These are the last words that Lord Śiva utters in the Īśvara Gītā. After Śiva departs, Nārāyaṇa says a few words of praise for Śiva, and then he too leaves the audience of sages. Here we see a concern to justify another apparent departure from the Bhagavad Gītā, the shift from understanding Kṛṣṇa or Viṣṇu as the highest god to the portrayal of Lord Śiva as supreme.[65] Through Śiva's insistence that he and Nārāyaṇa are one, the text attempts to preempt objections from worshippers of Nārāyaṇa. This is not unlike the strategies in the Bhagavad Gītā itself, which subordinates all other gods to Kṛṣṇa, the god of gods (*devadeva*). Kṛṣṇa is the ultimate recipient of all other gods' sacrifices:

When devoted men sacrifice
to other deities with faith,
they sacrifice to me, Arjuna,
however aberrant the rites.

I am the enjoyer
and the lord of all sacrifices;
they do not know me in reality,
and so they fail.[66]

Of course, Śaivas can employ the same strategy with regard to Viṣṇu and his incarnations. Chapter 11 the Īśvara Gītā does this, drawing upon the language of the above verses from the Bhagavad Gītā:

Those who sacrifice to other deities
for the enjoyment of pleasure
receive fruits according to those deities.
This much should be known.

But if people who are devoted
to other deities sacrifice to them
knowing them to be the same as me,
they too are actually freed.

So when someone completely abandons
other gods who are not the lord
and takes refuge in me, the lord,
one goes to the highest abode.[67]

There can be little doubt that the Īśvara Gītā borrows from the Bhagavad Gītā. But why does it do so? We should first dismiss the idea that its authors were lazy, unoriginal, or suffering from writer's block. It is more likely that the opposite is the case—certain parts of the Īśvara Gītā seem too original, seem to introduce ideas concerning yogic visualization exercises and worship of the Śiva *liṅga* that are too different from the Bhagavad Gītā. The authors of the Īśvara Gītā follow such novel sections with themes that every intelligent person will know immediately to be the same as the Bhagavad Gītā. These sections enhance the text's authority by showing that, in spite of the apparent novelty of some of the Īśvara Gītā's teachings, the two texts are in basic agreement in their major themes.

In the past ten years, historians of Indian religions have paid new attention to the early Śaiva sects, among them the Pāśupatas. One fact has become increasingly clear: The teachings of the Pāśupatas, the first recorded and most widespread of the Śaiva sects in ancient India, cannot simply be reduced to the teachings of the Pāśupata Sūtras, as some earlier scholars were wont to do. Recent work on an even earlier Pāśupata Purāṇa, the Skanda Purāṇa, has suggested that the differences between the rigid casteism and sexism of Kauṇḍinya's commentary on the Pāśupata Sūtras and the relative openness of the Pāśupata ideas expressed in the Purāṇas can be better understood by looking at the social and political history of the first millennium in India.[68] For example, it was the Pāśupatas who, between the third and sixth centuries CE, brought the worship of Śiva to Vārāṇasī, a city now famous as the holiest city for Śiva worshippers across India. In this second phase of Pāśupatism after the composition of the Pāśupata Sūtras, members of this group received considerable royal patronage and actively recruited lay supporters. Mendicant ascetics, such as Buddhist, Jain, and Pāśupata monks, required an outside source of food and material support, as their own codes of conduct prevented them from farming and most types of business.[69] Similar to the symbiotic relationship between early Buddhist monks and lay Buddhists, the Pāśupatas established a foothold as priests in temples across India, supported by lay devotees who sought Lord Śiva's grace and his aid in dealing with their everyday concerns. In the Pāśupatas' movement from the periphery to the mainstream of religious life in first millennium India, they let go of some of the extreme and forbidding aspects of the path described by Kauṇḍinya, such as the prohibition against talking to women and *śūdras*. A kinder, gentler Pāśupata teaching was born, and the Īśvara Gītā is perhaps its most famous exemplar.

However, not everyone accepted the movement from the periphery to the mainstream of these dreadlocked, ash-smeared yogis. This conflict is reflected in those other parts of the Purāṇas where Pāśupatas are shunned as dangerous heretics of the same sort as Buddhists and Jains. Members of established sects that understood Viṣṇu, not Śiva, to be the supreme god were not swayed by the inclusivism of the Īśvara Gītā. Although the new Pāśupata attitude in the Purāṇas of emphasizing the value rather than the deficiencies of Vaiṣṇava and Pātañjala

Yoga teachings is a departure from the harsh rhetoric of the Pāśupata Sūtras, the Īśvara Gītā too teaches that ultimately all liberation occurs by the grace of Śiva. But eventually, by the mid-second millennium of the Common Era, such disputes were "ancient history," so to speak. Late medieval Vaiṣṇava interpreters of the Purāṇas were willing to accept the teachings of the Īśvara Gītā, declaring them the same in essence as the Bhagavad Gītā. The attempt of the Īśvara Gītā's authors to downplay the more extreme and challenging aspects of their sect's history had basically succeeded. As a result the Īśvara Gītā became a text widely accepted and commented on by non-Śaiva authors. The Pāśupatas went from being one of the most reviled sects to being identified as one of the established *āstika,* or "affirmer," schools.[70] Today, when the Pāśupatas are remembered at all, they are remembered as just one colorful tile in the brilliant mosaic of Hinduism.

Notes on Translation

The Sanskrit language presents special challenges for a translator. Like Greek and Latin, it is an inflected language, so the order of words in Sanskrit is much less important to the meaning of a sentence than in English. There also are no rules in Sanskrit about "run-on sentences." As a result, a single sentence might go on for many pages, and a translator from Sanskrit into English often will have little choice but to break up a single sentence into several in English. Another issue is that for many Sanskrit words there is no single equivalent in English. Just as there is no single English word available to translate the German word *Schadenfreude* ("happiness at the misfortune of another"), Sanskrit is full of compound words that elude every attempt at a single-word English translation. I have done my best to seek a middle path between the type of extremely literal translation favored by specialists, which is often incomprehensible to an English reader without knowledge of Sanskrit, and a translation that so emphasizes readability in American English that the original meaning of the text is distorted beyond recognition.

The format of the Īśvara Gītā and similar works such as the Bhagavad Gītā and the Śvetāśvatara Upaniṣad may initially appear so foreign that it does not seem to qualify as what we think of as a "philosophical text." Although it may seem strange to Westerners, the idea of a fundamental division between philosophers and poets is seldom found in premodern India. Instead, major philosophers like Śaṅkara and Rāmānuja also were celebrated for their poetry. The Īśvara Gītā is a philosophical poem composed in two different meters. The most common is a meter containing four quarters of eight syllables each, for a total of thirty-two syllables per stanza. This meter, known as the *anuṣṭubh,* is the most common in classical Sanskrit. The other meter used by the Īśvara Gītā is the longer *triṣṭubh,* four quarters of eleven syllables for a total of forty-four syllables. The *triṣṭubh* is sometimes used to give a sense of heightened intensity. It is used in the Bhagavad Gītā in the climactic eleventh chapter where Kṛṣṇa gives Arjuna a vision of his absolute form, and similarly in chapter 5 of the Īśvara Gītā to depict Śiva's dance of cosmic creation and destruction.[71] I have chosen to adhere to a few metrical contraints in my translation of the Īśvara Gītā. I translate the *anuṣṭubh* sections into four-line stanzas containing four to twelve syllables per line. For the *triṣṭubh* verses of the Īśvara Gītā, I use eight-line stanzas of no more than nine syllables per line.[72] I hope that this alternation between four- and eight-line stanzas will give the reader a feel for the original Sanskrit meter without being unnecessarily distracting.

I have tried to be consistent in the way I translate Sanskrit philosophical and religious terms into English without being too mechanical. However, certain Sanskrit words, such as *dharma* and *yoga,* are just too complex and multifaceted to be successfully translated. I have left such words in the original Sanskrit, usually with a note in my commentary explaining how the term should be understood in its specific context. For the Pāśupata sect, the most important meaning of *yoga* is "union" of the self with Lord Śiva. Yet the Īśvara Gīta uses *yoga* in many other ways as well. For instance, it enumerates four different *yogas* ("spiritual paths"): *bhakti-yoga* (the *yoga* of devotion), *karma-yoga* (the *yoga* of action), *jñāna-yoga* (the *yoga* of wisdom), and *dhyāna-yoga* (the *yoga* of mental concentration).[73] I have made the choice not to use consistently gender-neutral language in this translation. With few exceptions, Sanskrit texts in premodern India were composed by men and intended primarily for their eyes and ears. The quintessential practitioner of yoga in the eighth century CE was male. However, unlike the Pāśupata Sūtras, the Īśvara Gītā nowhere expressly forbids women from the practice of yoga.[74]

Coming after the translation of the Īśvara Gītā in this book are commentarial notes explaining the ideas and language in many of the verses; the transliterated Sanskrit text of the Īśvara Gītā; a list of concordances noting parallel verses from the Bhagavad Gītā and Upaniṣads; and a glossary of Sanskrit terms and proper nouns. The edition of the Sanskrit text presented here is based on the critical edition published by the All-India Kashiraj Trust, with minor emendations.[75] Whatever readers' motivations for picking up this book, whether it be spiritual illumination, intellectual curiosity, or something else entirely, I hope they find what they seek in the Īśvara Gītā, Lord Śiva's Song.

Guide to Sanskrit Pronounciation

This guide to the sounds of the Sanskrit alphabet gives approximate American English equivalents. For more on Sanskrit phonology, readers may consult Robert Goldman and Sally Sutherland's *Devavāṇīpraveśikā: An Introduction to the Sanskrit Language*. (Berkeley: Center for South Asia Studies, 1999.)

Sanskrit Letter as in English

a b*u*t
ā f*a*ther
i s*i*t
ī mach*i*ne
u p*u*t
ū t*u*ba
ṛ bitt*er*
ḷ litt*le*
e g*a*te
ai *ai*sle
o sl*ow*
au c*ow*
k *k*ite
g *g*oat
ṅ si*ng*
c *ch*ill (not as in *c*are or re*c*eive)
j *j*ury
ñ ca*ny*on
ṭ hi*t* (tongue touching roof of mouth)
ḍ hi*d* (tongue touching roof of mouth)
ṇ fi*n* (tongue touching roof of mouth)
t *t*en (tongue touching teeth)
d *d*og (tongue touching teeth)
n *n*ew (tongue touching teeth)
p *p*it
b *b*all
m *m*attress
y *y*ellow
r *r*ecord (lightly trilled)

l *l*eopard
v *v*ery (almost sounds like w as in *w*all)
ś *sh*arp
ṣ fi*sh* (tongue touching roof of mouth)
h *h*ave
kh, gh, ch, jh, ṭh, ḍh, th, dh, ph, bh aspirated consonants, as in thic*k*-*h*ead, ju*gh*ead, ho*th*ouse, u*ph*ill, etc. (not as in wi*th*, *ph*one)

Suggestions for Further Reading

Brown, C. Mackenzie (ed. and tr.) (1998). *The Devi Gita: The Song of the Goddess.* Albany: State University of New York Press.

Bryant, Edwin F. (ed. and tr.) (2009). *The Yoga Sūtras of Patañjali.* New York: North Point Press.

Davis, Richard H. (1991). *Ritual in an Oscillating Universe: Worshiping Śiva in Medieval India.* Princeton: Princeton University Press.

Dimmitt, Cornelia and J.A.B. van Buitenen (ed. and tr.) (1978). *Classical Hindu Mythology: A Reader in the Sanskrit Purāṇas.* Philadelphia: Temple University Press.

Flood, Gavin (ed.) (2003). *The Blackwell Companion to Hinduism.* Maldon, MA: Blackwell Publishing.

King, Richard (1999). *Indian Philosophy: An Introduction to Hindu and Buddhist Thought.* Washington, D.C.: Georgetown University Press.

Olivelle, Patrick (ed. and tr.) (1996). *Upaniṣads.* New York: Oxford University Press.

Patton, Laurie L. (ed. and tr.) (2008). *The Bhagavad Gita.* New York: Penguin.

White, David Gordon (ed.) (2012). *Yoga in Practice.* Princeton: Princeton University Press.

Notes

1. For Patañjali, the highest stage of yoga is "absorption without support" (asaṃprajñāta samādhi), a type of meditation that does not take god as its focus (see Bryant 2009:70–2). By contrast, the Īśvara Gītā teaches that the highest yoga, beyond asaṃprajñāta samādhi, is absorption in Śiva.

2. The Bhagavad Gītā was composed between approximately the second century BCE and the second century CE (see Flood 1996:107, 123–7). The Kūrma Purāṇa, of which the Īśvara Gītā is a part, was composed around the eighth century CE (see Rocher 1986:184–6).

3. For instance, Bhagavad Gītā 13.13 is identical to Śvetāśvatara Upaniṣad 3.16. This same verse also appears at Īśvara Gītā 3.2: "It dwells in the world, enveloping everything, hands and feet everywhere, eyes, head, face, and ears everywhere." Part of this Upaniṣad's importance is that it foreshadows the type of inclusive monotheism that would become so prevalent in medieval Vaiṣṇava, Śaiva, and Śākta (Goddess-worship) traditions. For more on the Śvetāśvatara Upaniṣad, see Olivelle (1996:253–65).

4. For selected translations of some of the most important and influential sections of the Purāṇas, see Dimmitt and van Buitenen (1978).

5. Hindus who see Viṣṇu as supreme are known as Vaiṣṇavas, and those who understand Śakti (the Goddess) as supreme are known in Sanskrit as Śāktas. The Bhagavad Gītā, for instance, is understood as a Vaiṣṇava text insofar as Kṛṣṇa is understood by many as an incarnation (avatara) of Viṣṇu.

6. The 16th-century philosopher Vijñānabhikṣu suggests that because he has already written a commentary on the Īśvara Gītā, it would be redundant to write another on the Bhagavad Gītā. See Nicholson (2010:75).

7. Gandhi suggested that the poet who composed the Bhagavad Gītā did not see the "great consequences" of his own philosophical teachings. It was because of this that the Bhagavad Gītā appears to accept the violence of war (Gandhi 1965:49).

8. See Malinar (2009:54–225) for one recent theory of the "layers" of authorship in the Bhagavad Gītā.

9. Edgerton (1934:306).

10. Upadhyaya (2008: 521–3).

11. Ibid., 512.

12. For more on the Purāṇas' place in Indian religious history, see Doniger (1993).

13. Nilakantan (1989) counts at least twenty-six Gītās in the Mahābhārata and the Purāṇas.

14. The Devī Gītā ("Song of the Goddess") is a Gītā text that shows the influence of tantric concepts. See Brown (1998:1–29).

15. The word māyā appears five times in the Bhagavad Gītā (BhG 4.6, 7.14, 7.15, 7.25, 18.61). It is interesting to note that the word māyā does not appear in the Pāśupata Sūtras, though it does occur in other Śaiva philosophies, such as that of Śrīkaṇṭha (see Dasgupta 1975:65–129).

16. Miller (1986:121).

17. Īśvara Gītā 8.3, 8.7, 8.8. On the idea of māyā as a feminine force, see Pintchman (1994:198–200). On the androgynous form of Śiva known as Ardhanarīśvara ("The lord who is half woman"), see Goldberg (2002).

18. On the Bhagavad Gītā's influence on modern Hindu thinkers, see Minor (1986).

19. For more information on the renouncer perspective see Olivelle (1992:19–58).

20. It is important to note that the Bhagavad Gītā and Īśvara Gītā accept some of the traditional distinctions between classes (varṇas), for instance by describing the different livelihoods appropriate to the different varṇas (at Bhagavad Gītā 18.41–7).

21. The Īśvara Gītā follows closely the eight-limbed yoga scheme presented by Patañjali, in which celibacy (brahmacarya), non-acquisition (aparigraha), and non-harming (ahiṃsā) are among the "restraints," the first and most fundamental of the eight limbs. But such restraints are contrary to the pursuits of the traditional Brahmin priest, who was enjoined by the Vedas to father children, accumulate wealth, and engage in sacrifices that sometimes involved the killing of animals (see Bryant 2009:242–52).

22. Īśvara Gītā verse 1.27.

23. Bhagavad Gītā verses 6.10–14 discuss practical aspects of yoga.

24. The Mahābhārata classifies the Pāśupata doctrine as one of the "knowledges," along with "the Vedas" (vedāḥ), Sāṃkhya-Yoga, and Pañcarātra (see Dyczkowski 1988:19).

25. For instance, the Mīmāṃsā ritual theorist Kumārila Bhaṭṭa lists the Pāśupatas alongside Buddhists and Jains as a group whose teachings on dharma are unreliable (Hara 2002:18).

26. See Dyczkowski (1988:24).

27. Kauṇḍinya prescribes a purificatory ritual of bathing in ashes and breath exercises (prāṇayāma) that the Pāśupata yogi should practice whenever he sees urine, feces, a śūdra, or a woman (commentary on Pāśupata Sūtra 1.13; Chakraborti 1970:78–9). Kauṇḍinya's commentary is notoriously misogynistic. In the context of his discussion of celibacy, he describes women as "poison," and "the root of all evils" (commentary on Pāśupata Sūtra 1.9; Chakraborti 1970:66). Mark Dyczkowski notes that there is evidence of some Kṣatriyas being initiated into Pāśupatism; it is not clear how seriously to take Kauṇḍinya's insistence that only Brahmins can be Pāśupatas (Dyczkowski 1988:24).

28. See Sanderson (2005:158). This is expressed even more directly at Īśvara Gītā 11.67, which says that Pāśupata yoga is "beyond the stages of life" (atyāśrama).

29. See Kauṇḍinya's commentary on Pāśupata Sūtra 1.1 for a concise summary of Pāśupata theology (Chakraborti 1970:50–5).

30. Īśvara Gīta 7.18–20. It is remarkable that the idea of god's play (līlā), so common throughout the Purāṇas, does not appear in Pāśupata Sūtras or Kauṇḍinya's commentary on that text.

31. On the three stages of Pāśupata practice, see Flood (2003:207).

32. In conscious contradiction of Patañjali, Kauṇḍinya introduces ten restraints (yamas) for the Pāśupatas: non-harming (ahiṃsā), celibacy (brahmacarya), truthfulness (satya), non-transaction (asaṃvyavahāra), non-stealing (asteya), non-anger (akrodha), obedience to the teacher (guru-śuśrūṣā), purity (śauca), moderation in diet (āhāra-lāghava), and mindfulness (apramāda) (see Kauṇḍinya's commentary on Pāśupata Sūtra 1.9; Chakraborti 1970:61–77). This may be compared to the five restraints enumerated in Patañjali's Yoga Sūtra 2.30 (Bryant 2009:242–52). Just as the Pāśupata Sūtra presents itself as a fifth stage of life beyond the four stages of mainstream Hindu legal texts, it presents its ten restraints (yamas) and ten observances (niyamas) as going beyond the Yoga Sūtras of Patañjali.

33. See Kauṇḍinya's commentary on Pāśupata Sūtra 1.8 (Chakraborti 1970:60). On the Pāśupatas and dance, see Smith (2008:125–6) and Davidson (2002:223). Davidson also claims, "the Pāśupatas are the probable source for the employment of song and dance in the Buddhist forms of worship, which is ubiquitous in yoginī-tantra literature" (Ibid.).

34. See Ingalls (1962) and Hulin (1993). The ancient Cynics were said to live a simple life like that of a dog (the word "Cynic" may have come from the Greek word kunikos, meaning "dog-like"). Similarly, Pāśupatas are

instructed to have "the nature of a cow or a deer," because such animals were thought to have a high tolerance for physical and mental distress (Pāśupata Sūtra 5.18; Chakraborti 1970:165).

35. See Pāśupata Sūtras 3.12–17 (Chakraborti 1970:128–32).

36. See Kauṇḍinya's commentary on Pāśupata Sūtra 3.3 (Chakraborti 1970:123).

37. Pāśupata Sūtra 5.9.

38. Ibid., 5.30.

39. Ibid., 5.39–40.

40. "Those who have won [supposed] release through Sāṃkhya-Yoga, indeed all creatures from Brahman down to the animals, are considered 'beasts.'" (commentary on Pāśupata Sūtra 1.1; Sastri 1940:5). Note that the meanings of the terms sāṃkhya and yoga are different in the Bhagavad Gītā than in the Pāśupata Sūtras and the Īśvara Gītā (see Malinar 2009:70–79, Nicholson 2010:70–72).

41. For more on Advaita Vedānta's concept of nirguṇa brahman and its non-theistic philosophical position, see King (1999:213–6). It is important to note that the terms nirguṇa ("without qualities") and saguṇa ("with qualities") do not refer to the three guṇas of the Sāṃkhya philosophical tradition.

42. For those verses that appear to indicate that brahman is not beyond the gods, as when Kṛṣṇa describes himself as the "foundation" (pratiṣṭhā) of brahman at Bhagavad Gītā 14.27, Śaṅkara argues that the text must be read figuratively, rather than literally (see Gambhirananda 2006:589–90).

43. In many cases, the theistic Vedāntins were themselves influenced by Purāṇic sources such as the Īśvara Gītā, leading to a confluence of Vedanta and devotion (bhakti) not found among earlier Vedāntic commentators. For more on Rāmānuja's Vaiṣṇava interpretation of Vedānta see King (1999:221–8). On Śrīkaṇṭha's Śaiva commentary on the Brahma Sūtras, see Dasgupta (1975:65–95).

44. See Pāśupata Sūtra 1.13 (Chakraborti 1970:78).

45. See commentary on Pāśupata Sūtra 1.9 (Chakraborti 1970:66).

46. Īśvara Gītā 4.10–11, 11.104; Bhagavad Gītā 9.32.

47. Īśvara Gītā 4.10–11.

48. It is due to such discrepancies in Pāśupata texts that Dyczkowski suggests, "we must clearly distinguish between two basic types of Pāśupata teachings, namely, one that bases itself on Vedic "tradition, and another that runs counter to that tradition" (Dyczkowski 1988:24).

49. Kūrma Purāṇa 2.16.15.

50. Ibid., 2.21.34–35.

51. On the issue of ahiṃsā as a dividing line among Hindus, see Halbfass (1990:87–130).

52. Īśvara Gītā 11.14–15.

53. For more on the Pāśupata concept of ahiṃsā, see Hara (2002:67–76).

54. Laws of Manu 5.44; translated in Olivelle (2005:140).

55. Īśvara Gītā verses 11.4–7.

56. The central philosophical concept of the Madhyamaka Buddhist school of philosophy is "emptiness" (śūnyatā). The Īśvara Gītā's use of the

word śūnya should not, however, be taken as a reference to that school. For a better understanding of the term abhāva-yoga (yoga of non-being), it is useful to compare this description to descriptions of abhāva-yoga in the Śiva Purāṇa (7.2.37.7–10) and Liṅga Purāṇa (2.55.14).

57. Angelika Malinar suggests that a similar division between two types of yoga, one concerned with cessation (nirodha), the other with "the vision of God . . . as this self" is also present in the Bhagavad Gītā (see White 2012:64).

58. PABh 1.1 (Sastri 1940: 5).

59. The Pāśupata Sūtra's observances (yamas) are non-harming (ahiṃsā), celibacy (brahmacarya), truthfulness (satya), non-transaction (asaṃvyavahāra), non-stealing (asteya), non-anger (akrodha), obedience to the teacher (guru-śuśrūṣā), purity (śauca), moderation in diet (āhāra-lāghava), and mindfulness (apramāda). For more on the ten observances and ten abstentions, see Kauṇḍinya's commentary on Pāśupata Sūtra 1.9 (Chakraborti 1970:61–77).

60. Īśvara Gītā 11.11–12.

61. Edwin Bryant suggests this possibility in his recent commentary on Patañjali's Yoga Sūtas (Bryant 2009:87–99).

62. Īśvara Gītā 11.53–59.

63. Īśvara Gītā 11.67.

64. Īśvara Gītā 11.116–8.

65. Although in later times Kṛṣṇa was usually considered one among many incarnations of Viṣṇu, it is likely that the Bhagavad Gītā's authors considered Kṛṣṇa himself to be the highest god. For instance, the word "Viṣṇu" is used only four times in the Bhagavad Gītā (see Malinar 2009:163–86).

66. This translation of BhG 9.23–24 is from Miller (1986:86).

67. Īśvara Gītā 11.89–91.

68. See, for instance, Bisschop (2006:3–88) and Smith (2008:58–140).

69. For instance, Kauṇḍinya's commentary on the Pāśupata Sūtra 1.9 lists "non-transaction" (asaṃvyavahāra) as one of the ten restraints (yamas) (Chakraborti 1970:61–77).

70. For instance, the influential 16th-century catalogue of philosophies, the Sarva Darśana Saṃgraha ("Compendium of All Philosophical Schools") categorizes the Pāśupatas as an āstika philosophy. On the meaning and history of the terms āstika ("affirmer") and nāstika ("denier") see Nicholson (2010:166–79).

71. This section of the Īśvara Gītā is in conscious imitation, I believe, of the theophany of Kṛṣṇa in Bhagavad Gītā chapter 11, verses 15–50.

72. I borrow this strategy for marking changes between anuṣṭubh to triṣṭubh meter from Barbara Stoler Miller's translation of the Bhagavad Gītā (Miller 1986).

73. See Īśvara Gītā 4.24. At 11.72–3, the Īśvara Gītā lists only three (excluding dhyāna-yoga). Swami Vivekananda may have derived his famous scheme of "four yogas" from this verse.

74. Not only are women forbidden from initiation, but Pāśupata Sūtra 1.13 also states, "One should not talk with a woman or śūdra" (Chakraborti 1970:79). Because the Īśvara Gītā nowhere repeats this prohibition, however, it is unclear whether it applies here. Unlike the Pāśupata Sūtras, the Īśvara Gītā

states that it is possible for śūdras to be liberated (Īśvara Gītā 1.104). From this it is possible to infer that the Īśvara Gītā also has more liberal attitudes toward women than the Pāśupata Sūtras.

75. For variant readings of the Īśvara Gītā text that I present here, I encourage readers to consult the critical edition of the Kūrma Purāṇa (Gupta 1971:373–432). The Īśvara Gītā consists of sections 2.1–11 of the Kūrma Purāṇa.

TRANSLATION

LORD ŚIVA'S SONG

The Īśvara Gītā

Chapter One

The Arrival of the Gods

The sages said:

1. Sūta, you have spoken rightly
of the creation of the first man,
the expansion of the cosmos,
and the order of world-epochs.

2. You say that celibate students
engaged in *dharma* and constantly
devoted to the yoga of knowledge
should worship god, the lord of lords.

3. Please explain the supreme knowledge
whose sole object is *brahman*,
destroying the suffering of all rebirths
and allowing us to see the ultimate.

4. Lord, you have obtained
complete knowledge from Vyāsa,

who is Nārāyaṇa personified.
Therefore, we ask you again.

5. Sūta, bard of the Purāṇas,
listened to the sages' words.
Calling Lord Vyāsa to mind
he was about to speak.

6. At that very moment Vyāsa,
Kṛṣṇa Dvaipāyana himself,
arrived where the great sages
were holding their sacrifice.

7. Those brahmins bowed down
upon seeing Vyāsa, knower
of the Veda. His splendor was like
a dark cloud, his eyes like lotus leaves.

8. Seeing Vyāsa, Sūta threw himself
to the ground, straight as a stick.
Sūta walked around the teacher
and stood by his side, palms together.

9. Vyāsa inquired after the health
of Śaunaka and the other wise men.

They reassured the great sage
and arranged for him a proper seat.

10. Then mighty Lord Vyāsa,
son of Parāśara, asked them,
"Are there any difficulties with your
austerities, Vedic studies, or learning?"

11. Sūta bowed to his teacher,
that great sage, and said,
"Please explain to these wise men
the knowledge of *brahman*.

12. These calm ascetics are
sages engaged with *dharma*,
full of desire to listen.
Please explain as it truly is

13. the divine knowledge leading to freedom.
You told it to me in person.
Viṣṇu explained it to the wise men
long ago, in his tortoise form."

14. Hearing Sūta's request,
the sage Vyāsa, son of Satyavatī,

bowed his head to Śiva
and spoke these pleasing words.

Vyāsa said:

15. I will tell you what the god Śiva
himself said when questioned
long ago by the lords among yogis,
headed by Sanatkumāra.

16. Sanatkumāra, Sanaka,
Sanandana, and Aṅgiras,
along with Rudra and Bhṛgu,
the great scholar of *dharma*,

17. Kaṇāda, Kapila the yogi,
the great sage Vāmadeva,
Śukra, and glorious Vasiṣṭha,
all masters of mental discipline,

18. consulted one another,
their minds penetrated by doubt.
They practiced fearsome austerities
at holy Badarikā hermitage.

19. There they saw Nārāyaṇa,
the seer whose yoga was great,

the son of Dharma, immortal
and pure. Nara was with him.

20. They all praised him
with various hymns from the Vedas.
Full of devotion, the yogis bowed
to the one who knows yoga best.

21. The omniscient lord
who knew their wishes
asked them in a deep voice,
"What is the purpose of these austerities?"

22. Thrilled, they spoke to Nārāyaṇa,
eternal self of the universe,
the god whose arrival before them
signaled their achievement.

23. "We who speak of *brahman*
are sunken in doubt.
We approach you alone
for refuge, the highest spirit.

24. You know that highest truth.
You are the sage and omniscient lord,
the ancient unmanifest spirit,
Nārāyaṇa himself before our eyes.

25. There is no one who knows
other than you, supreme lord.
We are eager to listen,
So please cut off all of our doubts.

26. What is the cause of this whole universe?
Who is reborn time and time again?
What is the self and what is liberation?
What causes the cycle of rebirth?

27. Who is the lord who causes others
to be reborn? Who sees everything?
What is the highest *brahman*?
Please explain all of this to us."

28. After saying this, the sages saw
the highest spirit had cast off
his form as an ascetic,
and stood now in his own brilliance.

29. Shining, immaculate, embellished
with a halo of light, the god had
the brilliance of molten gold.
The mark of Śrī's beloved was on his breast.

30. Covered with light, in his hands
were a conch, discus, club, and bow.

For an instant Nārāyaṇa's
radiance made Nara invisible.

31. Just then the great Lord Śiva appeared,
crescent moon upon his forehead,
the terrifying one,
with kind intentions for the sages.

32. Seeing him, their minds were thrilled.
With devotion they praised the lord
of the universe, the three-eyed one
whose ornament is the moon:

33. "Hail, lord! Hail, great god!
Hail, Śiva, lord of beings!
Hail, lord of all sages,
recipient of our austerities!

34. Hail, thousand-formed one, self of all beings,
Impeller of the world-machine,
endless cause of the world's creation,
preservation, and destruction!

35. Hail, thousand-footed lord, delightful one
extolled by the greatest yogis!
Husband of the mother goddess,
supreme lord, we bow to you!"

36. After this praise, the three-eyed lord
felt affection for his devotees.
He embraced bristling-haired
Nārāyaṇa and spoke in a deep voice:

37. "Lotus-eyed one, why have
the great sages who speak of *brahman*
come to this place? Unwavering one,
what should I do for them?"

38. The god among gods,
Nārāyaṇa, gave ear to the lord's words.
He replied to the great god Śiva
who stood there with kind intentions.

39. "Lord, these sages are ascetics
who have wiped away all impurity.
With the desire for right knowledge
they have come to me for refuge.

40. If you are pleased with
these self-cultivated sages,
please explain that divine knowledge
here in my presence.

41. You know your own self.
Śiva, there is no one else who knows.

So you yourself should show
the self to the great sages."

42. Saying this, he gazed at Śiva,
whose emblem is the bull.
Disclosing Śiva's yogic power,
Nārāyaṇa spoke to the bulls among sages.

43. "Because you have now seen Śiva,
the great lord, trident in hand,
know yourselves truly
to have achieved your goal.

44. You may ask the lord of the universe,
who stands before your eyes.
And you, lord, please speak the truth
here in my presence."

45. After hearing Viṣṇu's words
the sages bowed to Śiva.
Headed by Sanatkumāra
they queried the great lord.

46. At just that moment a throne appeared
from the sky, divine, auspicious,
immaculate—something inconceivable,
as befits Lord Śiva himself.

47. The maker of all, self of yoga,
sat down there with Viṣṇu.
Great Lord Śiva shone, filling
the universe with his radiance.

48. The sages who spoke of *brahman*
saw Śiva, radiating brilliance,
first of the gods and lord
of them all, on that flawless throne.

49. They saw calm Śiva, his radiance
without equal. Those who are
steady in yoga see that lord
as the self inside themselves.

50. They saw the lord of beings
seated upon that throne.
From him comes the creation of beings.
Into him that creation dissolves.

51. They saw that lord seated
alongside Nārāyaṇa.
Everything is inside of him.
This world is not separate from him.

52. After their request, the blessed one
glanced at lotus-eyed Nārāyaṇa.

The supreme lord taught the sages
the unsurpassed yoga of his own self.

53. "All you blameless sages,
you whose minds are at peace,
listen to my true teaching—
the wisdom imparted by the lord."

Chapter Two

The Changeless Self

Lord Śiva said:

1. Twice-borns, this eternal knowledge
is my secret, and should not be uttered.
Even the gods do not know it,
though they strive for it.

2. Taking refuge in this knowledge,
the best of twice-borns become *brahman*.
Like the ancients who spoke of *brahman*,
they do not undergo rebirth.

3. The most secret of secrets, it
should be guarded with great effort.
I will now tell it directly to you
who speak of *brahman*, so full of devotion.

4. The self that is alone, self-contained,
calm, subtle, and eternal is

pure consciousness itself,
inside all beings, beyond darkness.

5. It is inner controller, spirit,
breath, and the great lord.
It is time, fire, and the unmanifest.
The revealed texts say it is all this.

6. The universe arises from it,
and into it the universe dissolves.
It is the magician who creates
manifold forms bound by magical power.

7. This mighty one is not reborn,
nor does it cause rebirth for others.
It is not this earth, not water,
not energy, wind, or sky.

8. It is not the breath, not the mind,
not the unmanifest, not sound or touch,
not form, taste, or smell, not the "I,"
not the doer, and not speech.

9. Best of twice-borns, it is not
the hands, feet, anus or genitals,
not the doer or enjoyer,

not matter or spirit,
not magical power or even breath.
In highest truth, it is consciousness.

10. The relation between light and
darkness is impossible. Likewise,
there is no relation of oneness
between the highest self and creation.

11. Here on earth, shadow and sunlight
have different characteristics.
So too, in highest truth, spirit
and created world are apart.

12. If the self were impure, infirm,
and changeable in its own nature,
it could not become liberated
even after hundreds of rebirths.

13. Sages deep in yoga see their own selves
according to the highest truth
as unchanging, free from suffering,
blissful in essence, and undying.

14. "I am the doer. I am happy.
I am suffering. I am weak. I am fat."

From the activity of the ego,
people project such thoughts onto the self.

15. Those who know the Veda say the self
is the witness, beyond matter.
It is the observer, imperishable,
pure, and standing everywhere.

16. Therefore ignorance is the cause of
rebirth for all embodied beings.
From ignorance, which is false knowledge,
spirit is conjoined with matter.

17. The self is eternally arisen,
self-luminous, all-pervading supreme spirit.
The ego's lack of discrimination
makes people think "I am the doer."

18. Sages who speak of *brahman* perceive
primeval matter, unmanifest
and eternal, seeing that as the cause.
Its nature is the good and the bad.

19. Even joined with matter, that self is still
unchanging and free from blemish.

People do not know that their nature
is actually imperishable *brahman*.

20. Suffering and other states come from
perceiving the self in that which is
not the self. All flaws, such as passion
and hatred, are caused by this confusion.

21. For the person who acts,
there are flaws of merit and demerit.
This is how it is. By force of this,
all are born into various bodies.

22. The self is eternal, all-pervading,
unchanging, and flawless. It is one,
divided through magical power,
not divided in its own nature.

23. So wise men say that in highest truth
there is only nonduality. Difference
comes from the nature of manifest things.
Magical power is located in the self.

24. The sky does not become dirty
through contact with smoke.

Sentiments from the organ of thought,
likewise, do not adhere to the self.

25. A pure, immaculate crystal shines
with its own brilliance. The self,
without stain, free from limiting
conditions, shines in the same way.

26. Clear-sighted people say that the essence
of this world is knowledge.
Ignorant people with wrong views
see the physical as its essence.

27. In its own nature the self is consciousness:
changeless, beyond qualities,
and all-pervading. People whose vision
is confused see it as physical form.

28. People perceive a pure crystal as red
when it is next to something
that is red. They perceive
the highest spirit in the same way.

29. Seekers of freedom should hear about it,
contemplate it, and meditate on it.

It is the imperishable, pure,
eternal, all-pervading, undying self.

30. When all-pervading consciousness
shines in the mind constantly,
without interruption,
then the yogi attains himself.

31. When he sees all beings
in his own self and he sees
the self in all beings,
then he attains *brahman*.

32. When, steady in meditation,
he sees no beings, he has
become one with the highest.
Then he is alone.

33. When all desires abiding
in his heart are banished,
then he has become immortal.
That learned one achieves peace.

34. When he sees the many states of beings
as abiding in the one,

their expansion coming only from that,
then he attains *brahman*.

35. When he sees that in highest truth
the self is alone and the entire world
is nothing but magical power,
then he is satisfied.

36. When he obtains the sole knowledge
of *brahman*—the only remedy
for the diseases of birth, old age,
and suffering—then he is Śiva.

37. Here on earth, rivers and streams
become one with the ocean.
Likewise the self becomes one
with imperishable, undivided *brahman*.

38. Therefore only knowledge exists,
not the created world, not rebirth.
Knowledge is concealed by ignorance.
From it, people become confused.

39. Such knowledge is stainless, subtle,
nonconceptual, and undying.

Everything else is ignorance.
That is how I understand knowledge.

40. I tell you that this highest *sāṃkhya*
is the supreme knowledge, the essence
of all the Upaniṣads. Yoga is
one-pointed mental focus on that knowledge.

41. Knowledge is produced by yoga,
and yoga proceeds from knowledge.
The person who has mastered yoga
and knowledge has nothing else to obtain.

42. Yogis attain the same state
attained by followers of *sāṃkhya*.
He who sees *sāṃkhya* and yoga
as one knows the truth.

43. Other yogis focus their minds
on lordly powers. The Vedas say
they sink into just those powers
and do not attain the self.

44. However, when his body perishes,
the master of knowledge and yoga

achieves the divine, unwavering,
all-pervading, great state of lordliness.

45. I am the self, the unmanifest,
the magician, the supreme lord
celebrated in all the Vedas, the
self of everyone, facing everywhere.

46. I possess all desires, all tastes, all smells.
I am free from old age and death.
With hands and feet everywhere,
I am the eternal inner controller.

47. Though without hands or feet, I am swift.
I am the grasper who resides in the heart.
Though without eyes, I see.
Though without ears, I hear.

48. I know this entire world
yet no one knows me.
Those who see the reality say that
I am the one, the great spirit.

49. Sages who see subtle things
know that the cause, supreme lordliness,

belongs to the self, which is
free from qualities and without stain.

50. Listen attentively, you sages
who speak of *brahman*! I will tell you
something that the gods, confused
by my magical power, do not discern.

51. I am not director of all things,
for in my own nature I am
beyond magical power. Yet wise men
know that I set that cause in motion.

52. Yogis who see reality
enter into union with me,
obtaining my most secret,
all-pervading, undying body.

53. My polymorphous magical
power falls into their control.
They obtain the highest purity,
nirvāṇa, union with me.

54. Greatest yogis, it is by my grace
that they do not return again,

not even after a billion cosmic cycles.
This is the teaching of the Vedas.

55. Those who speak of *brahman*
should give this knowledge
of *sāṃkhya* and yoga that I teach
only to sons, pupils, and yogis.

Chapter Three

The Unmanifest Lord

Lord Śiva said:

1. From the unmanifest came time,
primeval matter, and the supreme spirit.
The whole world was born from these three,
so the world consists of *brahman*.

2. It dwells in the world,
enveloping everything,
hands and feet everywhere,
eyes, head, face, and ears everywhere.

3. It appears to possess all qualities
and all senses, yet is free of them all.
Supporting all things, it is eternal bliss,
the unmanifest, free from duality.

4. Without any object of comparison,
its range is beyond the means of knowledge.

The abode of all things, supreme immortality,
beyond mental construction or semblance,

5. undivided, yet appearing as divided,
it is eternal, fixed, and unchanging.
It is without qualities, the highest space.
This is the knowledge the wise understand.

6. It is the self of all beings.
It is the external, the internal, the supreme.
It is I, all-pervading and calm,
the highest lord whose essence is knowledge.

7. I, whose form is unmanifest,
pervade this entire world.
All beings dwell in me.
He who knows this knows the Vedas.

8. The two principles are called
primeval matter and spirit.
Their uniter is time, the supreme,
stated to be beginningless.

9. These three stand fixed in the unmanifest,
without beginning or end. The wise

know that that my form is identical to
the three, yet different from them.

10. The one who gives birth to the entire world,
from the principle of intellect to the
individual elements, is called matter.
She is the deceiver of all embodied beings.

11. The spirit, standing with matter,
experiencing the *guṇas* of matter,
is called the twenty-fifth principle
because it is free from ego.

12. The first evolute of matter
is named the "great one."
It is the knower, possessing the power
of cognition. Out of it comes the ego.

13. The "great one" is one only.
Those who reflect on the principles
say it is also the ego. They say it is
the individual, the inner self.

14. It causes knowledge of all happiness
and suffering in human lifetimes.

Its nature is cognition and
and the mind is its assistant.

15. Because of its lack of discrimination,
the spirit undergoes rebirth.
This lack of discrimination
is from the connection of matter with time.

16. Time creates beings
and time destroys them.
All are subject to time,
yet time is subject to no one.

17. It is eternal and interior,
regulating all things.
It is proclaimed Lord Breath,
the omniscient one, the highest spirit.

18. The learned say that the mind
is superior to all the senses,
the ego higher than the mind,
the intellect higher than the ego.

19. The unmanifest is higher than the intellect,
the spirit higher than the unmanifest.

Lord Breath is higher than the spirit.
The entire world belongs to him.

20. Space is higher than breath,
and Lord Agni is beyond space.
He is I, all-pervading and calm,
the highest lord whose essence is knowledge.
There is no being higher than me.
Those who know me are freed.

21. No being in the world is eternal,
whether mobile or immobile,
except for me, the one, the unmanifest,
the great lord whose nature is space.

22. That is I, the divine magician.
Joined with time, I eternally
emit and absorb the entire world,
which is made up of magical power.

23. Time, whose nature is endless,
creates and impels the entire world
only due to my presence.
This is the teaching of the Vedas.

Chapter Four

The God of Gods

Lord Śiva said:

1. Listen, you collected sages
who speak of *brahman*! I will tell you
the glory of the god of gods
who sets this world in motion.

2. I cannot be known to men
through manifold austerities,
through charity, or through sacrifice,
without incomparable devotion.

3. Lordly sages, I am all-pervading
and dwell in the interior of all beings.
People do not know me,
the witness of all.

4. This entire world is inside me,
and I am the supreme, inside all beings,

facing all directions. I am the founder,
provider, and the fire at the end of time.

5. Sages, dwellers in the highest heaven,
Brahmā, the Manus, Śakra,
and the superpowerful beings—
none of them see me.

6. The Vedas constantly praise me
as the one, the supreme lord.
Brahmins sacrifice to me as Agni
by various Vedic rites.

7. All the worlds revere me, as does
Brahmā, patriarch of worlds.
Yogis meditate on me, the lord,
the god who rules all beings.

8. I am the recipient of all sacrifices
and the one who bestows their fruits.
Taking the form of all the gods,
I am everywhere, the self of everyone.

9. Wise, virtuous scholars of the Veda
see me in this world.

I am always near to those
who worship me with devotion.

10. Virtuous brahmins, warriors,
and merchants worship me.
I grant them the state of bliss,
the supreme abode.

11. Even servants and others of low birth
who pursue forbidden occupations
are in time freed and joined to me
if they are full of devotion.

12. Those devoted to me are not annihilated.
All of their stains are wiped clean.
In the beginning I made this promise:
my devotee does not perish.

13. The fool who scorns my devotee
scorns the god of gods.
One who honors him with devotion
is always honoring me.

14. A disciplined person who gives
a leaf, a flower, fruit, or water

to please me is my devotee.
He is considered dear to me.

15. I created Brahmā, the supreme one,
at the beginning of the world.
I gave him all of the Vedas,
which emanate from my self.

16. I am the immortal teacher
of all the yogis. I am protector
of the virtuous and destroyer
of the enemies of the Vedas.

17. I free yogis from the entire cycle
of death and rebirth here in the world.
Free of this entire cycle,
I am its only cause.

18. I alone am the destroyer.
I am the creator and maintainer.
As the magician, the magical power
of world-deception belongs to me.

19. Mine too is that highest power
that is praised as "knowledge."

Using it to destroy illusory power,
I rest in the hearts of yogis.

20. I am the impeller of all powers
and the one who restrains them,
the foundation of them all
and the reservoir of immortality.

21. One power inside of all beings,
consisting of and controlled by me,
takes the form of Brahmā
and creates the manifold world.

22. Another vast power of mine
becomes Nārāyaṇa, the endless,
all-encompassing lord of the world.
That power sustains the world.

23. My third great power
destroys the entire world.
Named "time," it is made up
of darkness. Its form is Rudra.

24. Some discern me through meditation,
others through knowledge,

some through the yoga of devotion,
still others through the yoga of action.

25. Of all the devotees,
the one I prefer, the dearest to me,
is one who constantly gratifies me
through knowledge, not otherwise.

26. The other three types of devotees
who long to gratify me
certainly also attain me,
and they too are not reborn.

27. I unfold this whole world
made of primeval matter and spirit.
The entire world dwells in me
and is set in motion by me.

28. Sages, I am not the director.
I direct the entire world
only as I rest in the highest yoga.
One who knows this becomes immortal.

29. I regard this entire world as
existing by its own nature.

It was created by time, the blessed one
who is the lord of the great yoga himself.

30. The wise say in learned texts
that "yoga" means magical power.
The "yogi" is that lord of yoga,
the blessed great god, the mighty one.

31. The supreme one is called "great"
because he is beyond all of the principles.
He is the blessed Brahmā, the great
immaculate one who is made up of *brahman*.

32. There is no doubt: one who knows me,
lord among lords of the great yoga,
is joined to me in the yoga that is
without conceptual constructions.

33. I am he, the god, the director,
resting in the highest bliss,
the yogi who dances perpetually.
The knower of the Veda knows this.

34. This most secret knowledge is in
all the Vedas. It should be given

only to one who tends the sacred fire,
who is mentally pure and righteous.

Chapter Five

The Lord's Dance

Vyāsa said:

1. After the lord, the highest god,
said this to the yogis,
he danced, showing them
his supreme lordly form.

2. They saw the master, the great god,
a supreme storehouse of light,
dancing with Viṣṇu
in the immaculate sky.

3. In the sky they truly saw
the lord of all beings, known
by yogis with disciplined minds
who know the reality of yoga.

4. The sages saw the dancing one himself.
This whole world belongs to him.

It is made up of magical power.
He sets it in motion.

5. They saw him, the dancing one.
By recalling him and his lotus feet,
people are freed from fear,
which arises out of ignorance.

6. They saw that yogi. Those who are
free from fatigue, breath subdued,
calm, and full of devotion—
such people see him as pure light.

7. They saw Rudra the liberator
in the sky. Gracious and
loving to his devotees, quickly
he frees them from ignorance.

8. The god with a body of a thousand heads,
a thousand feet, and a thousand arms,
with matted hair and a half-moon
fixed at the crown of his head,

9. wearing the skin of a tiger,
one enormous hand gripping a trident,
the other hand with a club,
his three eyes Sūrya, Soma, and Agni,

10. enveloping the entire universe with
his own radiance and abiding in it,
invincible, with horrible fangs
and the brilliance of ten million suns,

11. standing inside and outside the universe,
outside, interior, and beyond,
emitting blazing fire and
consuming the entire world—
they saw that god dancing,
the lord who is creator of all.

12. The great god whose yoga is great,
the divine god of the gods,
the master of beasts, the lord,
the undying light of lights,

13. large-eyed bearer of the Pināka bow,
cure for those sick from worldly existence,
the essence of time, the destroyer of time,
the god among gods, the great lord,

14. husband of Umā, many-eyed one,
supreme and full of the bliss of yoga,
abode of knowledge and renunciation
whose yoga of knowledge is eternal,

15. rich with the eternal lordly powers,
the foundation of *dharma*, unobtainable,
honored by Indra and Viṣṇu and
celebrated by the groups of great sages,

16. foundation of all powers,
lord among lords of the great yoga,
the highest *brahman* of the yogis
celebrated by them through yoga,
dwelling in the heart of yogis yet
concealed through yoga's magical power,

17. creator of the entire world,
free from disease, Nārāyaṇa
joined in union with the lord—
the ones who spoke of *brahman* saw him.

18. Seeing that this form of the lord
had the nature of Rudra and Nārāyaṇa,
the ones who spoke of *brahman*
realized that they had attained their goal.

19. Now Sanatkumāra,
Sanaka, and Bhṛgu,
Sanātana

and Sanandana,
Rudra, Aṅgiras,
Vāmadeva, and Śukra,
the great sage Atri,
Kapila, and Marīci,

20. seeing Rudra, ruler of the world,
whose left side is Viṣṇu
of the lotus navel,
meditated with him
in their hearts;
they bowed down
and folded their hands
on their foreheads.

21. Uttering the syllable Oṃ
they glanced at the god
sequestered in a cavern
in their inner bodies.
Their minds full of bliss,
they praised him
with the words
of the Veda.

The sages said:

22. "We bow to you—
the one lord,
the ancient person,
Rudra, the lord of breath
whose yoga is infinite,
the wise one inside our hearts,
the purifier
made up of *brahman*.

23. Meditating on you
dwelling immovable
inside their bodies,
calm, disciplined sages see you—
the womb of the Vedas,
immaculate and golden,
the supreme seer,
higher than the high ones.

24. The producer of the world
was produced from you.
You, the self of all beings,
are the infinitesimal atom,
the smallest of the small,
the greatest of the great.
All of the holy ones
speak only of you.

25. Hiraṇyagarbha,
the inner self of the world,
the ancient person,
was born from you.
Coming into existence
emitted by you,
he emits the entire world
by your rule.

26. You generated
all the Vedas;
they will issue
back into you.
We see you,
cause of the world,
dancing
in our hearts.

27. You are the one
who turns this wheel of *brahman*.
You are the magician,
the one lord of the world.
We bow and take refuge in you,
the essence of yoga.
the master of consciousness,
the celestial dance.

28. We see you dancing
in the highest sky
and meditate
on your supremacy—
the self of all beings,
entering into many forms,
experiencing again and again
the bliss of *brahman*.

29. The syllable Oṃ
refers to you,
the seed of liberation.
You are the imperishable one
secretly ensconced in matter.
In this world, the holy ones
speak of you as the truth
whose light shines by itself.

30. All of the Vedas
praise you constantly.
Sages whose flaws are gone
bow down to you.
Ascetics who are calm,
devoted to truth,
and established in *brahman*
enter into you, the best one.

31. The Veda is one, endless,
with many branches.
It communicates knowledge
of only you—your form is one.
Those who take refuge in you,
the Veda's object,
have eternal peace.
Others do not.

32. You are the husband of Pārvatī
and the beginningless mass of light.
You are Brahmā and Viṣṇu,
the supreme one, the best.
After you experience
the bliss of your self,
you lie down in your light,
unmoving and eternally free.

33. You, the one Rudra,
create everything in this world.
In your multiple forms
you protect the whole world.
At its end, the world
disappears into you alone.
We bow to you,
taking refuge in you.

34. They call you the one,
the seer, the sole Rudra,
breath, the great one,
Hari, Agni, the lord,
Indra, death,
wind, intelligence,
the founder, Āditya,
and the multiform one.

35. You are the imperishable,
the supreme object of knowledge.
You are the final resting place
of the entire world.
You are the undying protector
of the perpetual *dharma*.
You are the highest spirit,
the eternal one.

36. You alone are Viṣṇu.
You are four-faced Brahmā.
You alone are Rudra,
the blessed supreme lord.
You are the world-navel,
matter, the foundation.
You are the lord of everything,
the highest lord.

37. They say you are the one,
the ancient person
the color of the sun
who is beyond darkness—
pure consciousness,
unmanifest and inconceivable,
the sky, *brahman*, emptiness,
matter, and the unqualified.

38. You are the one in whom
the entire world shines;
You are undying, stainless,
and single in form.
Moreover, your form
is inconceivable;
inside of it
reality shines forth.

39. We all bow to you,
seeking refuge in you—
Rudra, the lord of yoga
whose powers are endless,
the final goal, the purifier
whose body is the Veda.
Great lord, ruler of beings,
be gracious to us!

40. By recalling
your lotus feet,
the seed of all rebirths
is destroyed.
Restraining our minds
and prostrating our bodies,
we beg the one lord
to be gracious.

41. Homage to you who are
being and being's source,
to you who are time,
the whole, and Hara!
Homage to you,
matted-haired Rudra!
Homage to you, Agni!
Homage to you, Śiva!"

42. Then the blessed one, the god
with matted hair who rides the bull,
withdrew his highest form and
returned to his mundane state as Bhava.

43. Seeing Bhava, lord of past and future,
standing there as before

with the god Nārāyaṇa,
the amazed sages spoke these words:

44. "Blessed lord of past and future
whose emblem is the bull,
after seeing your highest form
we are satisfied, eternal one.

45. From your grace comes
our constant faith in you alone,
the supreme stainless one,
the highest lord.

46. Auspicious one, we now wish
to hear of your glory again
as it truly is,
eternal and supreme."

47. Giving ear to their request,
the one who grants success in yoga
glanced at Nārāyaṇa
and spoke in a deep voice.

Chapter Six

The Glory of Lord Śiva

Lord Śiva said:

1. Listen, all you sages.
I, the supreme one, will tell you
of the glory of the lord
known by knowers of the Veda.

2. I am the one creator,
protector, and destroyer
of the entire world.
I am the eternal self of all beings.

3. I am the father,
the inner controller of all things.
All things dwell inside of me,
yet I am situated nowhere.

4. The supernatural form of mine
that you just saw, wise ones,

was a simulacrum I displayed
through my magical power.

5. I am situated in the middle
of all states of existence
and I set the whole world in motion.
This is my power of action.

6. Through this the universe moves
in accord with its own nature.
I am time, setting in motion
the whole composite world.

7. Bulls among sages, I create
the whole world with one of my parts.
With another form I destroy it.
This is my twofold character.

8. Without beginning, middle, or end,
I impel the principle of magical power
and agitate spirit and primeval matter
at the beginning of creation.

9. The universe is born from the union
of these two principles. As the intellect

and the other principles progress,
my radiance is revealed.

10. The sun god Hiraṇyagarbha,
witness to the entire world,
impeller of the wheel of time,
was also born from my body.

11. At the beginning of the cosmic cycle
I gave him my divine lordly power,
the eternal yoga of knowledge,
and the four Vedas that I created.

12. By my command, the god Brahmā,
taking on my state of being,
himself always wields
my divine lordly power.

13. Four-faced Brahmā,
omniscient maker of all worlds,
sends forth creation by my command.
Yet he originates from me.

14. Eternal Nārāyaṇa,
undying sustainer of worlds,

is my sublime form
engaging in protection.

15. Rudra, destroyer of all beings,
the mighty one whose essence is time,
perpetually reabsorbs the worlds
by my order. He too is my bodily form.

16. Agni, the bearer who brings
oblations to the gods, offerings
to the ancestors, and does the cooking,
is also impelled by my power.

17. By command of the lord,
Agni, the blessed universal one,
burns up all day and night
the food that has been eaten.

18. By command of the lord,
Varuṇa, bull among gods,
source of all the waters,
brings the entire world to life.

19. The one who dwells
inside and outside of beings,

the god Wind, supports
their bodies by my order.

20. Soma, who makes men live
and grants immortality
to the gods, proceeds
impelled by my command.

21. By the rule of the self-born one,
Sūrya constantly illuminates
the entire world with his brilliance
and spreads the rains.

22. Śakra, lord of all immortals,
ruler of the world, granting fruits
to those who sacrifice,
proceeds by my order.

23. The god Yama, scion of the sun
who punishes the wicked,
acts regularly in this world
by command of the god among gods.

24. Kubera, overseer of all wealth,
bestower of riches,

also always proceeds
by the command of the lord.

25. Nirṛti, king of all demons,
the god who dispenses
the fruits of dark activities,
always proceeds by my command.

26. Īśāna too, lord of the bands
of goblins and ghosts,
dispensing fruits of enjoyment
to devotees, is under my command.

27. Vāmadeva, pupil of Aṅgiras,
foremost in Rudra's bands of followers,
eternal protector of yogis,
proceeds by my command.

28. Gaṇeśa, guide to *dharma*,
worshipped by the entire world,
creator and remover of obstacles,
also proceeds by my instruction.

29. Mighty Skanda, best among those
who know *brahman*, general

of the army of the gods, is impelled
by the rule of the self-born one.

30. The lords of created beings,
great sages like Marīci,
create manifold worlds
only by the supreme one's command.

31. Śrī, wife of Nārāyaṇa,
giving great prosperity
to all beings,
proceeds by my grace.

32. The goddess Sarasvatī,
who bestows great speech,
is also impelled to set out
by the command of the lord.

33. The goddess Sāvitrī follows
the command of god.
When remembered, she rescues
all people from horrible hells.

34. Pārvatī, the highest goddess,
also moves by my word.

When she is discerned in meditation,
she presents knowledge of *brahman*.

35. Endless Śeṣa, of infinite greatness,
king of all the immortals,
bears the world on his head
by the command of god.

36. Agni, eternal destroyer,
takes the form of a horse
and drinks up the entire ocean
at the command of the lord.

37. The fourteen Manus,
famous in this world
for their energy, protect
all creatures by my command.

38. The Ādityas, Vasus,
Rudras, Maruts, Aśvins,
and all the other gods
are governed by my rule.

39. The Gandharvas, Garuḍas, Ṛkṣas,
Siddhas, Sādhyas, Cāraṇas,

spirits, demons, and goblins all stand
under the rule of the self-born one.

40. The *kalā*, *kāṣṭhā*, moment,
muhūrta, day, night, season,
fortnight, and month exist
under the rule of the lord of progeny.

41. The *yugas* and ages of Manu
are under my dominion,
as are the *paras*, the *parārdhas*,
and all the other divisions of time.

42. The four classes of beings,
both inanimate and animate,
proceed from the command
of god, the highest self.

43. All of the hells, upper regions,
and universes proceed
from the dominion
of the self-born one.

44. The countless universes
of the past, along with

all the things everywhere
within them, and so too

45. all the universes that will be,
and the things inside of them,
always fulfill the order
of the supreme, highest self.

46. Earth, water, fire, wind,
space, mind, intellect,
and primal matter, the first element,
proceed under my command.

47. Magical power, womb of all worlds,
deceiver of all embodied beings,
also eternally comes forth
from the command of the lord.

48. The self, called the supreme spirit,
the god of embodied beings,
eternally proceeds
from the command of the lord.

49. Knowledge, which cuts through
the thicket of confusion

and reveals the supreme abode,
also follows the great lord's command.

50. My power is the world's essence.
I set in motion the entire world
and it dissolves into me.
What else is there to say?

51. I am the blessed one, the lord,
the eternal self-luminous light,
the highest self, supreme *brahman*.
Besides me there is nothing.

52. I have taught you this,
the highest knowledge.
The person who knows it
is freed from the bonds of rebirth.

Chapter Seven

The Master of Beasts

Lord Śiva said:

1. Listen, all you sages,
to the majesty of the supreme one.
Knowing him, a person is liberated
and does not undergo rebirth.

2. My supreme abode is *brahman*,
higher than the highest,
undying, indivisible, and firm—
eternal bliss without mental constructions.

3. Among those who know *brahman*
I am self-born Brahmā, facing all directions.
Among those who possess magical power
I am the ancient undying god Hari.

4. Among yogis I am Śambhu;
among women, the mountain king's daughter.

Among the Ādityas I am Viṣṇu;
among the Vasus, the god of fire.

5. Among Rudras I am Śaṅkara,
and among birds, Garuḍa.
Among elephant kings I am Airāvata,
and among warriors, Rāma.

6. Among the sages I am Vasiṣṭha,
and among the gods, Indra.
Among the craftsmen I am Viśvakarman,
and among the immortals' foes, Prahlāda.

7. Among sages I am Vyāsa,
among the troops, Gaṇeśa.
Among heroes I am Vīrabhadra,
among the accomplished ones, wise Kapila.

8. Among mountains I am Meru,
and among heavenly bodies, the moon.
Among weapons I am the thunderbolt,
and among vows, truthfulness.

9. Among serpents I am lord Śeṣa,
and among generals, I am Skanda.

Among stages of life I am the householder,
and among lords, I am the great lord Śiva.

10. Among *kalpas* I am the great *kalpa*,
and among *yugas*, the *kṛta yuga*.
Among *yakṣas*, I am the god of wealth,
and among the lords of troops, Vīraka.

11. Among the progenitors I am Dakṣa;
among all the demons, Nirṛti.
Among the mighty ones I am wind;
among the continents, Puṣkara.

12. Among kings of beasts I am the lion,
and among devices, the bow.
Among the Vedas I am the Sāma,
and among ritual formulas, the Śatarudrīya.

13. Among all of the mantras I am the Sāvitrī,
and among the secret ones, Oṃ.
Among hymns, I am the hymn of the first man,
and among chants, the Jyeṣṭhasāma.

14. Among all those who know the meaning
of the Veda, I am self-born Manu.

Among countries, I am the land of *brahman*;
Among holy places, Vārāṇasī.

15. Among sciences, I am the science of the self;
among knowledges, the lord's supreme knowledge.
Among elements, I am space,
and among beings, death.

16. Among bonds, I am magical power.
Among those who tally, I am time itself.
Among goals, I am liberation.
Among the supreme, I am the highest lord.

17. You should also understand
any other being in this world
who is full of radiance and power
as my radiance made manifest.

18. All selves that undergo the cycle
of rebirth are called "beasts."
I am god, their master. The wise
know me as the "master of beasts."

19. In my play, I ensnare those beasts
using the fetters of magical power.

Those who speak of the Veda call me
the one who frees the beasts.

20. There is no liberator of those
ensnared in the fetters of magical power
other than me, the highest self,
the immortal ruler of beings.

21. The twenty-four principles, action,
illusory power, and the three *guṇas*—
these, and the afflictions that bind beasts,
are the beast-master's fetters.

22. Mind, intellect, ego, space, air,
water, fire, and earth—these are
the eight productive principles.
The others are the products.

23. Hearing, touching, seeing,
tasting, and smelling, the fifth;
anus, genitals, hands, feet,
and tongue, known as the tenth;

24. sound, contact, form,
taste, and smell too;

these twenty-three principles
derive from matter.

25. The twenty-fourth, primeval matter,
unmanifest, possessing the *guṇas*,
is without beginning, middle, or end.
It is the cause of the entire world.

26. Purity, agitation, and inertia
are called the three *guṇas*.
Sages know that unmanifest matter
is the equilibrium of these three.

27. Purity is knowledge, inertia is ignorance,
and agitation is said to be a mixture.
The seers know that the imbalance of *guṇas*
comes from error in the intellect.

28. *Dharma* and *adharma*—these are
the two bonds known as fetters.
When surrendered to me,
actions that bind lead to freedom.

29. Ignorance, egoism, attachment,
aversion, and fear of death—

sages call these the afflictions,
unshakable fetters that bind the self.

30. It is said that magical power
is the cause of these fetters.
That is original unmanifest matter,
the power that resides in me.

31. He is original matter, primeval,
and he is spirit too.
He, the eternal God among gods,
is the intellect and the other evolutes.

32. He is the bond
and the creator of bonds.
He is the fetter
and he is the beasts.
He knows everything,
yet none know him.
They call him the first,
the ancient spirit.

Chapter Eight

The Hidden Lord

Lord Śiva said:

1. Bulls among brahmins, I will tell you
another most secret teaching.
With this teaching, one crosses over
the terrible ocean of death and rebirth.

2. I am made up of *brahman*—
calm, eternal, pure, and undying.
I alone am called the blessed one,
the sole highest lord.

3. Great *brahman* is my womb.
That is where I place the seed.
It is the source named magical power,
and from it the entire world is born.

4. From it were born primeval matter,
spirit, also called the self,

intellect, ego, subtle elements,
gross elements, and sense organs.

5. From it came the golden egg
whose brilliance equals million suns.
Great Brahmā was born there
and invigorated by my power.

6. All the many other
living beings are made up of me,
but deluded by my magical power
they do not see me, their father.

7. Magical power is the supreme womb
of the forms that are born
in the wombs of all beings.
Sages know that I am the father.

8. The wise one who recognizes me
as inseminator, father, and ruler
does not become deluded
in any of the worlds.

9. I am the master of all sciences,
the highest lord of beings, blessed,

whose form is the syllable Oṃ.
I am Brahmā, lord of progeny.

10. He who sees the highest lord
abiding equally in all beings,
immortal within mortals—
he is the one who truly sees.

11. Seeing the lord situated
everywhere equally,
he himself does not injure the self,
so he goes the highest way.

12. Discerning the seven subtle principles
and the great lord with his six limbs,
knowing the use of primeval matter,
he goes to the highest *brahman*.

13. Sages say that
these are the six limbs
of the great lord,
who is all-pervading:
Omniscience, contentment,
beginningless wisdom, independence,
power that never wanes,
and power that is without end.

14. The sages say that these
are the seven subtle principles:
the five subtle elements,
the mind, and the self.
Matter, the primordial one,
is the material cause.
When the self is in its employ,
that is known as bondage.

15. In the Vedas,
the power hidden in matter
is called the cause
and the womb of the Vedas.
Beyond that power
is the single supreme one,
the great lord, the spirit
whose form is truth.

16. He is Brahmā, the yogi,
the highest self, the great one,
the ancient one who pervades space
and is known through the Vedas.
He is the one Rudra,
death, the unmanifest,
the one seed, the entire world,
the one and only god.

17. Some call him one,
others call him many.
Some say he is the one self,
while others say otherwise.
He is the smallest of the small,
the greatest of the great.
Those who know the Vedas
proclaim him the great god.

18. The wise one who knows god
as dwelling in secret,
the supreme ruler,
the ancient spirit
whose form is the world, golden,
the highest way of the wise—
That person abides
beyond the intellect.

Chapter Nine

Brahman's Powers

The sages said:

1. If the highest lord is partless, pure,
eternal, and free from activity,
how can the world be your form?
Please tell us this, great god.

Lord Śiva said:

2. Twice-borns, I am not the same as the world,
yet without me the world cannot exist.
The cause here is magical power,
which depends on me.

3. Magical power, resting on the unmanifest,
is a power without beginning or end.
This created world came from the unmanifest,
and magical power is its cause.

4. Sages say the unmanifest is the cause.
It is bliss and eternal light.
I am the highest *brahman*,
and besides me there is nothing.

5. Hence those who speak of *brahman*
have determined that the world is my form.
They proclaim this teaching
in terms of oneness and multiplicity.

6. Twice-borns, I am that supreme *brahman*,
the highest eternal self.
It is said that I, *brahman*, am uncaused.
Therefore, the self is flawless.

7. Magical power and the other powers
are infinite, fixed within the unmanifest.
The unmanifest, which is eternal and
located in heaven, shines alone.

8. Joined with the powers it appears as divided,
but in its nature it is indivisible.
By means of one of those powers,
beginningless, endless union with me occurs.

9. A person has superhuman attainments
by one power, yet by another they disappear.
That which is without beginning,
middle, or end is joined with ignorance.

10. That is the supreme unmanifest one,
embellished with a brilliant halo.
It is the supreme eternal radiance,
the highest abode of Viṣṇu.

11. Upon that the entire world
is woven and interwoven.
It is the whole world.
Knowing this leads to freedom.

12. Not reaching it, words turn back
together with the mind.
Knowing it as the bliss of *brahman*,
one is afraid of nothing at all.

13. I know that great spirit
who is the color
of the sun god,
beyond darkness.
Knowing that spirit,

the wise person is freed
and attains eternal bliss,
becoming *brahman*.

14. That supreme,
of which nothing is higher,
the one light among lights,
standing in heaven—
the wise person who knows
that this is the self
attains the self's bliss,
becoming *brahman*.

15. It is undying, impenetrable,
its body hidden,
the immortal bliss of *brahman*,
the entire world's abode—
so say the brahmins
who are established in *brahman*.
After going to it
one does not return again.

16. With knowledge of that,
the radiance that is
like a ray of light

flashing golden
in the highest space,
wise men perceive
the shining sky,
the immaculate abode.

17. Then the wise men
see the highest one,
experiencing again and again
the self within themselves.
The supreme one, great
and self-illuminating,
is this lord, the blessed one,
full of the bliss of *brahman*.

18. The one god is
hidden in all beings,
all-pervading, the self
inside of all beings.
The wise men who perceive
only him as the one
have eternal peace.
Others do not.

19. The blessed one, all-pervading,
all faces, all heads, all throats,

rests secretly in the hearts of all beings.
There is no object of desire besides him.

20. Bulls among sages, I have taught you
this majestic wisdom.
It must be guarded with special care.
It is difficult even for yogis to grasp.

Chapter Ten

Brahman and the Lord

Lord Śiva said:

1. *Brahman* is unmarked, unique, and unmanifest.
It has been established that it is the *liṅga*,
the self-luminous supreme reality
located in highest space.

2. The unmanifest cause is
the imperishable supreme abode.
Wise people regard it as
pure knowledge without qualities.

3. The Vedas say that those established in *brahman*,
who have taken on its state of being
and who always resolve to tranquility,
see the *liṅga* as that highest *brahman*.

4. Bulls among sages, otherwise
it is impossible to see me,

because there is no other knowledge
by which one knows the supreme.

5. Only wise people know this,
the highest knowledge.
Everything else is ignorance,
since the entire world is magical power.

6. Learned people say this knowledge,
which is pure, subtle, undying,
and free from mental constructions,
is just that self of mine.

7. Those who see the self as multiple
also see that supreme one,
for they understand the one undying truth
and abide in the highest state of being.

8. Whether they see me as one or many,
those who see me with devotion,
the lord and highest reality,
are known to have that as their essence.

9. They see before them their own self,
the highest lord. Eternally blissful

and free from mental constructions,
he is truth embodied. This is how it is.

10. Established in their own selves,
calm within the highest unmanifest one,
they enjoy the supreme, all-pervading
bliss that has *brahman* as its essence.

11. This is the highest freedom,
the best union with me.
It is *nirvāṇa,* oneness with *brahman,*
and aloneness. The seers know this.

12. So, only one supreme, auspicious thing
is without beginning, middle, and end.
That is the lord, the highest god.
By knowing him, one becomes free.

13. Sun does not shine in this world,
nor the moon,
nor the stars,
nor fire and lightning.
This whole world is always
bright with his light.
His eternal light shines
true and unwavering.

14. It shines as
eternally risen consciousness
free from mental constructions,
pure, great, and supreme.
Those who speak of *brahman*
regard it as the intimate,
eternal, unwavering reality.
It is the lord.

15. All the Vedas say
that the spirit is eternal bliss,
immortal, pure,
and the embodiment of truth.
Those who ascertain
the meaning of the Veda
meditate on that lord
with the syllable Oṃ.

16. He is not earth,
not water, not mind,
not fire, not breath,
not air, not space,
not even the intellect,
consciousness, or its opposite.
In the middle of highest space
the god Śiva shines alone.

17. I have told you the
highest secret,
the nectar of knowledge
hidden in all the Vedas.
The pious yogi
who knows the secret
should constantly practice yoga
in a solitary place.

Chapter Eleven

The Highest Yoga

Lord Śiva said:

1. Now I will explain the highest yoga,
most difficult to attain.
With that yoga, sages see the self
as the lord, luminous like the sun.

2. Immediately the fire of yoga
burns down the whole cage of evils.
Pure knowledge arises, leading directly
to *nirvāṇa* and supernormal powers.

3. Knowledge is produced by yoga
and yoga proceeds from knowledge.
The great lord is pleased with one
who has mastered yoga and knowledge.

4. Those who are yoked to this yoga on me,
whether once daily, twice daily,

three times daily, or all the time,
should be known as the "great lords."

5. But yoga is known to be of two kinds.
The first is considered the yoga
of non-being. The other is the
great yoga, the very best of all yogas.

6. The yoga in which one's own essence
is known to be empty, free from all
false appearances, is named the yoga
of non-being. Through it, one sees the self.

7. The yoga in which one discerns the self
as eternally blissful, free from blemish,
and united with me is called
the great yoga of the supreme lord.

8. All the other yogas discussed
by the yogis in their many books
are not worth one-sixteenth
a part of the yoga of *brahman*.

9. The yoga in which the liberated
see before their eyes that the universe

is the lord himself—this is considered
the supreme yoga among all the yogas.

10. Those who reject the lord do not see me,
the one, though they may practice yoga
hundreds and thousands of times
with disciplined minds.

11. Breath control, meditation,
sense withdrawal, concentration,
absorption, restraints, observances,
and posture—Best of sages,

12. yoga is the one-pointed focus
of the mind on me through suppression
of other mental activity.
I have just told you its eight means.

13. Non-harming, truthfulness, non-stealing,
celibacy, and non-acquisition,
in brief, are called the restraints.
They purify the minds of human beings.

14. The great sages define non-harming
as not causing pain anywhere

to any living being, whether through
physical action, thoughts, or speech.

15. There is no *dharma* higher than non-harming.
It is the greatest happiness. But harming
when following scripture's injunction
should be considered non-harming.

16. Through truthfulness one obtains everything.
Everything has its foundation in truthfulness.
Twice-borns define truthfulness as
the practice of telling things as they are.

17. Taking the possessions of others
by stealth or by force is stealing.
Through abstaining from that comes
non-stealing, the means to *dharma*.

18. Renouncing sexual intercourse
in actions, thoughts, and speech,
in all times, places, and circumstances,
is called celibacy.

19. Not willfully accepting possessions,
even in an emergency,

is called non-acquisition.
Maintain it with great effort.

20. Austerity, Vedic study, contentment,
purity, and worship of the lord,
in brief, are called the observances.
They grant success in yoga.

21. Those who practice austerity say
the highest austerity is emaciation
of the body through the extended fast,
the lunar penance, and so forth.

22. Recitation of the Upaniṣads,
the Śatarudrīya, and the syllable Oṃ
is what the wise call Vedic study.
It purifies the human disposition.

23. There are three kinds of Vedic study:
the voiced, the unvoiced, and the mental.
Those who know the meaning
of the Veda say the last kind is best.

24. That which generates verbal understanding
clearly in others who are listening

is called voiced Vedic study.
Now the definition of the unvoiced:

25. Merely moving the lips without generating
verbal understanding in another person
is unvoiced recitation. It is
a thousand times better than the voiced.

26. They know this as mental recitation:
concentration on the whole text
in sequence of its words and syllables
without the movement of the lips.

27. When a person always thinks
that whatever comes along by chance
is enough, the sages call it contentment.
It is characterized by happiness.

28. Best of twice-borns, purity is declared
to be twofold: external and internal.
The external is done with earth and water.
The internal is purification of the mind.

29. Worship of the lord is
unshakable devotion to Śiva

through praise, remembrance, and worship,
done in speech, mind, and body, respectively.

30. Now that restraints and observances
have been explained, learn about breath control.
"Breath" is wind that originates in the body.
"Control" means its suppression.

31. There are three types of breath control:
higher, lower, and middle.
Each of these three is also
of two types: seeded and unseeded.

32. The suppression of the breath
for twelve beats is the weak,
for twenty-four beats is the middle,
and for thirty-six beats is the higher.

33. The weak causes perspiration,
the middle causes trembling,
and the higher causes levitation.
Bliss is greatest with the last one.

34. The wise say that the "seeded" is
accompanied by mental recitation.

"Unseeded" is not. In this way
yogis define breath control.

35. With restrained breath one should recite
the Gāyatrī mantra three times
preceded by *Oṃ bhūr bhūvaḥ svaḥ*.
This is declared to be breath control.

36. Those who practice yoga with
disciplined minds say in all learned texts
that breath control consists of
expiration, inspiration, and retention.

37. Through continuous breathing out,
there is expiration. After its cessation,
there is inspiration. The state of
equilibrium is called retention.

38. Virtuous ones, sense withdrawal is
the restraint of the sense organs.
By their own nature, they would
move toward the objects of sense.

39. Concentration is fixing the mind
on a place such as the heart-lotus,

the navel, the forehead,
or the peak of a mountain.

40. The intellect's continued activity
resting in a single place, unmixed
with other mental activity,
is what the wise know as meditation.

41. Absorption is cognition whose form
is one and the same as the thing itself,
without a support in any place at all.
It is the best of the means of yoga.

42. Concentration is said to be
twelve times as valuable as breath control,
meditation twelve times concentration,
and absorption twelve times meditation.

43. Posture, consisting of the *svastika*,
lotus, and half-lotus postures,
is called the best means
of all the means of yoga.

44. Best of Brahmins, sitting
after putting the tops of both feet

on top of one's thighs is
the lotus, the best posture.

45. Most virtuous ones,
sitting after putting one foot
on one thigh is the half-lotus,
the best means of yoga.

46. Sitting after putting the soles
of both feet inside one's own
knees and thighs is called
the svastika, the supreme posture.

47. Even a mere glimpse of yoga
is impossible at the wrong places
and times: near fire, in water,
where there are piles of dried leaves,

48. in a place full of animals,
a cremation ground, a decrepit cowshed,
a crossroads, a noisy or dangerous place,
a place with many anthills,

49. in a place that is inauspicious, full of
wicked people, or mosquito-infested.

One should not practice when the body
is ill or the mind disturbed.

50. In a secluded, pleasant place,
in a mountain cave, on the bank
of a river, in a holy place,
in the sanctuary of a god,

51. in a pleasant, attractive house devoid of
people and animals—there the yogi
should constantly yoke the self
in yoga, with me as his final goal.

52. After bowing to the best of yogis,
to their disciples, to Gaṇeśa,
to his teacher, and to me, the yogi
should practice yoga with a collected mind.

53. Binding himself in the *svastika*,
lotus, or half posture, his gaze
resting evenly on the tip of his nose,
with eyes slightly open,

54. calm and free from fear, he renounces
this world consisting of magical power.

He concentrates on the supreme lord,
the god who resides in his own self.

55. He then visualizes a lotus twelve
fingers long from the root of his topknot.
It is beautiful, blooming from the bulb
that is *dharma*. Its stalk is knowledge,

56. the lordly powers its eight petals.
It is completely white. Renunciation
is its seed-cup. In that seed-cup he should
visualize a sublime golden treasure.

57. Consisting of all of the powers,
directly they call it Oṃ, the divine
eternal syllable, the unmanifest,
surrounded by a network of rays.

58. There he should think of
a pure, supreme, eternal light.
In that light he places his own self,
which is identical to it.

59. He meditates on the lord, highest cause,
standing in the middle of space.

At last, becoming the all-pervading
lord himself, he visualizes nothing.

60. This is the most secret meditation.
Now I will describe another:
visualizing in the heart the supreme
lotus that was previously described,

61. he visualizes the self, the doer,
brilliant as fire, as the spirit,
the twenty-fifth principle, in the form
of a flame in the middle of the lotus.

62. He should visualize the highest self
as the pure sky in the middle
of that lotus, as the eternal principle
expressed by Oṃ, the unwavering Śiva,

63. as the unmanifest, hidden in nature,
the supreme unsurpassed light.
Then he should visualize the supreme principle,
flawless, the support of the self.

64. He should visualize the great lord
who is uniform, eternal, consisting of the self,

who has purified all the principles
with the syllable Oṃ. Alternatively,

65. placing himself in me,
the immaculate highest abode,
washing his own body
with the water of knowledge,

66. having my self, constituted by me, he takes
the ashes of the *agnihotra* sacrifice
and smears them over his entire body,
reciting the mantra that begins
with the word "fire." He should visualize
in himself the lord whose essence is pure light.

67. This Pāśupata yoga is for the liberation
of creatures from their fetters. The Vedas
declare it the essence of all the Upaniṣads,
transcending the stages of life.

68. It is the highest of secrets,
leading to union with me.
It is taught for those twice-borns
who are devoted and celibate.

69. The limbs of the vow are specified as
celibacy, non-harming, patience,

purity, austerity, self-control,
contentment, truthfulness, and affirmation.

70. Even lacking just one of these,
his vow is broken. Therefore,
full of his own good qualities,
he should take up the vow to me.

71. Free from passion, fear, and anger,
constituted by me, taking
refuge in me, purified by this yoga,
many people attain my being.

72. I serve them depending on
the way they approach me.
So one might worship me, the supreme lord,
by means of the yoga of knowledge,

73. or by means of the yoga of devotion,
with complete renunciation. One who
is always pure might worship me
with a mind that is yoked to wisdom.

74. One who surrenders all actions,
begging for alms and practicing
non-acquisition, attains union with me.
This is the secret that I impart.

75. One who has no hatred for any being,
who is friendly and compassionate,
who has no possessiveness or ego,
who is devoted to me, is dear to me.

76. The yogi who is always content,
whose self is controlled, whose resolve is firm,
whose mind and intellect are fixed on me,
who is devoted to me, is dear to me.

77. One whom the world does not scorn
and who does not scorn the world,
who is free from elation, anger,
fear, and anxiety, is dear to me.

78. One who is impartial, pure, skillful, and
dispassionate, whose ill temper has gone,
who has given up all undertakings,
who is full of devotion, is dear to me.

79. One who regards blame and praise equally,
who is silent, content with whatever comes,
who has no home, whose mind is steady,
who is devoted to me, will reach me.

80. One who is committed to me,
even if constantly performing

all actions, attains the supreme
eternal abode by my grace.

81. One who surrenders all actions to me
in his mind and takes me as his highest goal,
becoming free from desire and greed,
should approach me as his lone refuge.

82. Abandoning attachment to action's fruits,
he is always satisfied and independent.
Even when engaged in action,
he is not bound by action at all.

83. One who is free from desire,
whose mind is disciplined, renouncing
all acquisitions, performing actions
only with his body, attains that highest abode.

84. For one who is content with whatever
comes along by chance, who is beyond
the dualities, acting just for my favor,
action destroys the cycle of rebirth.

85. His mind on me, bowing to me,
sacrificing to me, taking me as his goal,
knowing me as the supreme lord,
this lord among yogis will reach me.

86. Those whose thoughts are on me,
constantly teaching each other
and always talking about me,
should attain union with me.

87. For those who always strive in this way,
I destroy all the darkness
that follows their actions
with the shining lamp of knowledge.

88. I bring security in yoga
to those people who are always striving,
whose thoughts are on me,
constantly worshipping me in this world.

89. Those who sacrifice to other deities
for the enjoyment of pleasure
receive fruits according to those deities.
This much should be known.

90. But if people who are devoted
to other deities sacrifice to them
knowing them to be the same as me,
they too are actually freed.

91. So when someone completely abandons
other gods who are not the lord

and takes refuge in me, the lord,
one goes to the highest abode.

92. Abandoning affection for sons and family,
without sorrow and without possessions,
a renouncer should worship the supreme lord
in the form of the *liṅga* until his death.

93. I grant supreme lordly power
in a single lifetime
to those who always worship the *liṅga*,
completely abandoning enjoyments.

94. The *liṅga's* essence is the highest bliss.
It is the sole existent, free from blemish.
Consisting of knowledge, it is all-pervading,
standing in the hearts of yogis.

95. Disciplined devotees who meditate
according to the method taught
may worship the supreme lord
in that *liṅga* anywhere at all.

96. Meditating on the lord's *liṅga*
in water, in fire, in the sky,
in the sun, in a jewel, and so forth,
one should worship the lord.

97. This whole world is made of the *liṅga.*
This whole world rests upon the *liṅga.*
Therefore, in the *liṅga* one may worship
the eternal lord anywhere at all.

98. For the ritualists, the *liṅga* is in fire.
For the learned, it is in water, sky, or sun.
For fools, it is only in wood or stone.
But for yogis, it is in the heart.

99. If a renouncer who is full of love but
has not yet cultivated wisdom
recites the syllable Oṃ, the essence
of *brahman,* for his entire life,

100. or if a solitary twice-born
recites the Śatarudrīya
with a disciplined mind until his death,
he will go to the supreme abode.

101. Or if a wise, collected person
lives in Vārāṇasī until his death,
he too will go to that supreme abode
through the grace of the lord.

102. At their time of death
I give all embodied beings there

the highest knowledge,
freeing them from their fetters.

103. Following all duties according to caste
and stage of life, committed to me,
he gains knowledge in that very lifetime
and goes to the auspicious abode.

104. Twice-borns, all people who reside there,
even the lowborn and those who come
from evil wombs, pass beyond the cycle
of rebirth by the grace of the lord.

105. Twice-borns, there will be obstacles for those
whose thoughts are overwhelmed by evil.
Therefore, for liberation
take constant refuge in *dharma*.

106. This secret of the Vedas
should not be given to anyone
other than the righteous, celibate
student who is full of devotion.

Vyāsa said:

107. After explaining his own
incomparable yoga, the lord

spoke to Nārāyaṇa, who had been
sitting there free from discomfort.

108. "I have uttered this wisdom for the benefit
of those who speak of *brahman*.
You should share this auspicious wisdom
with pupils whose minds are calm."

109. Just after saying this,
the unborn lord spoke
to the great yogis for the benefit
of all twice-born devotees: "Twice-borns,

110. following my instruction,
you too should impart my wisdom
to all devoted pupils
according to rule.

111. I, Lord Śiva, am this Nārāyaṇa.
Of this there is no doubt. Those who see
no difference between him and me
should be granted the highest wisdom.

112. This highest form of mine,
named Nārāyaṇa, peacefully

dwells in the selves of all beings.
It is called the imperishable.

113. But some people think otherwise,
seeing difference in the world.
They do not apprehend me,
and are born again and again.

114. There is no rebirth for people
who see this Viṣṇu
as being one with me,
the unmanifest Lord Śiva.

115. Therefore, you should regard Viṣṇu,
the beginningless, endless,
imperishable self, as me alone,
and worship in that way.

116. Those people go to terrible hells
who see me otherwise,
thinking that he and I are different gods.
I do not abide in them.

117. I liberate those who take refuge in me:
the fool and the scholar,

the Brahmin and the dog-cooker,
but not one who reviles Nārāyaṇa.

118. Therefore, to give me pleasure
my devotees should
praise him and bow to him,
the highest spirit, the great yogi."

119. Śiva, bearer of the Pināka bow,
spoke these words and embraced Viṣṇu.
He then disappeared in front of
the entire audience of onlookers.

120. And blessed Nārāyaṇa assumed
the excellent appearance of an ascetic,
casting off his highest form
and taking leave of those yogis:

121. "By the grace of the great supreme lord
in person, you have acquired
the immaculate knowledge
that destroys the cycle of rebirth.

122. Lords among sages,
all of you free from afflictions,

go and convey the supreme one's
wisdom to your virtuous students.

123. You should give this lordly wisdom
in particular to the devoted,
calm, righteous brahmin
who tends the sacred fire."

124. Saying this, the self of the universe,
the most learned about yoga
among yogis, the great yogi
Nārāyaṇa himself disappeared.

125. Bowing down to the great lord
who is first among gods and to Nārāyaṇa
who is first among beings, the sages too
dispersed to their own lands.

126. Lord Sanatkumāra, that great sage,
gave the lord's teaching
to Saṃvarta. He in turn
gave it to Satyavrata.

127. Sanandana, best of yoga practitioners,
transmitted it to the great sage Pulaha.

The lord of progeny Pulaha
then transmitted it to Gautama.

128. Aṅgiras gave it to Bharadvāja,
who knew the Veda.
Kapila gave it to Jaigīṣavya
and also to Pañcaśikha.

129. My father Parāśara,
who knew all of reality, obtained
that highest knowledge from Sanaka,
and Vālmīki received it from Parāśara.

130. The god created from the bodies
of Satī and Bhava told it to me
long ago. The great yogi Vāmadeva
is the Rudra who carries the Pināka bow.

131. Lord Nārāyaṇa, Viṣṇu himself,
offspring of Devakī,
gave this supreme teaching
to Arjuna in person.

132. The incomparable wisdom
I received from Rudra Vāmadeva

produced in me a special devotion
to the mountain-dwelling lord.

133. I took refuge specifically in Rudra,
the protector, mountain-dweller,
the unshakable lord of beings,
the god of gods who bears the trident.

134. You too, with all your wives
and all your sons—proceed for refuge
in Śiva, the delightful one,
the god who rides the bull.

135. Turn toward the benevolent one.
Through the yoga of action,
by his grace, worship the great lord
adorned with ash, protector of cowherds.

136. Hearing this, the sages led by Śaunaka
bowed down to the great Lord Śiva,
eternal and unshakable,
and to Vyāsa, son of Satyavatī.

137. With pleased minds they spoke
to mighty Vyāsa, who is

bristling-haired Viṣṇu personified,
great lord of all the worlds.

138. "By your grace, unwavering devotion
to Śiva, the bull-emblemed protector,
is now born in us. Such devotion is
hard even for the gods to attain.

139. Best of sages, explain to us
the incomparable yoga of action
that will allow seekers of freedom
to gratify the blessed lord.

140. Vyāsa, in your presence
let Sūta hear the words the lord used
to summarize the *dharma*
for the protection of all the worlds.

141. The god of gods Viṣṇu, in tortoise form,
explained it when Śakra and the sages
asked him long ago, when he churned
the nectar out of the ocean."

142. Hearing this, Vyāsa,
son of Satyavatī, taught the sages

the eternal yoga of action
that Kṛṣṇa had taught with focused mind.

143. One who constantly reads
this conversation between Śiva
and the sages headed by Sanatkumāra
will be freed from all evils.

144. One who recites this
to pure twice-borns intent on celibacy
or who ponders its meaning
goes the highest way.

145. And one who hears this constantly,
joined to devotion with a firm vow,
is liberated from all evils
and is exalted in the world of Brahmā.

146. Therefore, wise people,
especially brahmins,
should read, hear, and reflect on it
with all effort forever.

Commentarial Notes

Chapter 1

1.1 The Īśvara Gītā begins with the sages addressing the bard Sūta, also known as Lomaharṣaṇa. Although the name "Sūta" is not included in this verse, I supply it for clarity.

"The first man" refers to Svāyaṃbhuva, the first human being created during this particular world-epoch (*manvantara*). His name means "descendent of the self-born one." "Self-born one" (*svayaṃbhū*) is an epithet given to the creator god.

1.2 "Celibate students" refers to *brahmacārins* (here called *varṇins*), students who have undertaken study of the Vedas and have yet to marry. This is first of the four stages of life (*āśramas*) according to many Hindu legal texts.

"The lord of lords" (*īśvareśvara*) is the one whom all other gods acknowledge as highest. According to the Īśvara Gītā, that god is Śiva.

1.6 "Kṛṣṇa Dvaipāyana" ("Island-born Kṛṣṇa") does not refer to the god Kṛṣṇa of the Bhagavad Gītā, but rather to Vyāsa, the mythical sage and author of the Mahābhārata and Purāṇas. Verse 1.4 asserts, however, that Vyāsa is himself a form of Nārāyaṇa/Viṣṇu.

1.8 Circumambulation is a traditional way of honoring a teacher or worshipping a god. It should always be done clockwise.

"Palms together" refers to the *añjali*, a gesture of greeting and respect still widely used in India and Tibet today.

1.11 Sūta's request here is an implicit answer to Vyāsa's question at 1.10. The difficulty these sages face is that they cannot ascertain the true nature of *brahman*.

1.13 This is a reference to the story of the tortoise (*kūrma*) incarnation of Viṣṇu, when the gods and demons churned the ocean of milk using a mountain as a churning stick, balanced on the back of a giant tortoise at the bottom of the sea. The Īśvara Gītā is itself a section of the Kūrma Purāṇa, a text that takes its name from Viṣṇu's tortoise avatar.

1.15 Here begins the narration by the sage Vyāsa. Vyāsa narrates the text until 11.137, when his pupil Sūta speaks again.

According to R.C. Hazra (1987:62–71), this is the point in the text at which the later author or authors of the Īśvara Gītā introduce Śiva, transforming what was previously a Vaiṣṇava text into a text that understands Śiva as the highest god. Hazra's hypothesis helps to explain some of the sudden transitions and puzzling interactions between the gods Nārāyaṇa and Śiva in chapter 1.

1.17 "Rudra" in this verse refers to a sage named Rudra, not to the wrathful incarnation of the god Śiva.

1.18 Badarikā, known today as Badrinath, is a locale in the Himālayas. It has historically been an important pilgrimage center both for Vaiṣṇavas and Śaivas.

1.19 Nara and Nārāyaṇa are twin incarnations of Viṣṇu, sometimes identified with Arjuna and Kṛṣṇa of the Bhagavad Gītā. They are also closely associated with Badarikā, as at Bhāgavata Purāṇa 3.4.22.

1.21 "Austerities" translates *tapas,* which can literally mean "heat" (from the verbal root *tap,* "to heat up"). Through the practice of austerities, yogis become powerful by storing up heat in their bodies.

1.22 The arrival of the god Nārāyaṇa indicates that the sages' austerities have been a success. Translated more literally, it is Nārāyaṇa himself who is described as "signaling [their] achievement" (*siddhisūcaka*).

1.23 I have translated the noun *brahmavādin*, which appears frequently throughout the Īśvara Gītā, as "one who speaks of *brahman*." It also might be appropriate to translate as "one who speaks of the Vedas," but because discussion of the true nature of *brahman* is one of the central themes of the Īśvara Gītā, I have chosen the former translation. Also see the note at 4.9 for *vedavādin*.

1.24 "The ancient unmanifest spirit" refers to the Sāṃkhya philosophical school's concept of *puruṣa,* often translated "person." According to Sāṃkhya, the *puruṣa* is pure consciousness. Any passion or conceptual content ascribed to it is actually part of the realm of matter (*prakṛti*). Complete freedom comes from the disunion of spirit and matter, and is known in Sāṃkhya as "aloneness" (*kaivalya*). For a summary of Sāṃkhya philosophy, see King (1999:166–89).

"Highest spirit" (*puruṣottama*) is also a common epithet for god, denoting that *puruṣa* who has never been deluded into thinking that he is the same as *prakṛti*.

1.25 This could mean that Śiva is the only one who knows the highest truth mentioned at 1.24. It also could be interpreted more metaphysically: In the entire universe, there is only one "knower" (*vettṛ*), Śiva.

1.28 The god Nārāyaṇa gives the sages a glimpse of his divine form. Previously he was disguised as a human ascetic (*tāpasa*).

1.29 "Śrī's beloved" (*śrīvatsa*) is an epithet of the god Viṣṇu. In this case the word refers to a special mark Viṣṇu bears on his chest, also called the *śrīvatsa*.

1.30 Instead of "covered with light," this also can be interpreted as "accompanied by the goddess Śrī."

1.31 Śiva's abrupt entrance is slightly puzzling. One interpretation is that the human sage Nara here reveals his true form to be Śiva, just as at 1.28 Nārāyaṇa reveals his divine form. This abrupt transition could be due to a textual interpolation (see note at 1.15).

"The Terrifying One" is an approximate translation of "Rudra," another common name for Śiva. Although Śiva can be terrifying, he arrives here with the desire to bestow his grace (*prasāda*) upon the sages.

1.33 "Lord of beings" (*bhūtapati*) can mean the lord of all beings (*bhūtas*), but it also has a specific mythological significance. In his terrifying form as Rudra, Śiva is the lord of the ghosts (*bhūtas*) who haunt places such as cremation grounds.

1.34 Here the world is likened to a machine (*yantra*). Śiva sets this machine in motion. A similar metaphor of the phenomenal world as a machine operated by god appears at Bhagavad Gītā 18.61. For a survey of some of the machines used in premodern India, see Raghavan (1952). Implicit in the metaphor in the Bhagavad Gītā and here is that individual beings are cogs in a great machine, with god as its operator—possibly denying humans free will.

1.38 As at 1.31, Śiva's desire to bestow his grace (*prasāda*) is emphasized here.

1.41 As at 1.25, this could be interpreted metaphysically: There is only one knower in the entire universe.

This verse plays on the multiple meanings of the Sanskrit word *ātman,* which can mean the conventional self (the mind, the body, and the senses), the ultimate self, or can simply be used as a reflexive pronoun ("himself," "yourself"). Compare similar wordplay on *ātman* in the Bhagavad Gītā (6.5, 6.20, 10.15, 13.29).

1.42 Although it is unclear from the language here whose "yogic power" (*yoga-siddhi*) Nārāyaṇa is explaining, in this context it would make sense that it is Śiva who is being extolled. The word *siddhi* is also ambiguous—in the context of the yoga of the Pāśupata sect it often means superhuman power attained though yoga, yet it also can simply mean "accomplishment" or "success."

"Bulls among sages" (*muni-puṅgavān*) is a stock phrase meaning "best of sages." In this verse the poet uses it to play on an epithet of Śiva, "one whose emblem is the bull" (*vṛṣabhadhvajam*).

1.44 Although it may seem strange that Nārāyaṇa asks Śiva to speak truthfully, the sixteenth-century commentator Vijñānabhikṣu points out that Śiva has a reputation for dishonesty in his teachings—some of his discourses are teachings of darkness (*tāmasa śāstras*), designed to delude the wicked. According to Vijñānabhikṣu's commentary, it is only because he is in the presence of Viṣṇu, who formally requests that he tell the truth, that we can be certain that Śiva's teaching in the Īśvara Gītā is correct. Hence, Nārāyaṇa's emphasis here and at 1.40 that Śiva should speak "just in my presence" (*mamaiva sannidhau*).

1.46 All of the epithets used to describe Śiva's throne—divine, free from flaws, auspicious (*śiva*), inconceivable—are epithets that can be applied to the god Śiva himself.

Chapter 2

2.1 The term *twice-born* (*dvija*) can refer to any of the highest three classes (*varṇas*): priests, warriors, or merchants. In this text, it primarily refers to the priestly class (the brahmins).

"My secret" (*ātmaguhya*) also could be translated "the secret of the self."

2.4 "Darkness" (*tamas*) refers to one of the three *guṇas* of the system of Sāṃkhya philosophy. There are three *guṇas*, colored white, red, and black, that can be translated as purity (*sattva*), agitation (*rajas*), and inertia (*tamas*), respectively. These three *guṇas* constitute the material world (*prakṛti*), and all aspects of the material world can be understood as being an admixture of these three *guṇas*. For more, see King (1999:166–89).

2.5 "Spirit" (*puruṣa*) is one of the twenty-five principles (*tattvas*) of Sāṃkhya philosophy. It is separate from the other twenty-four, which consist of primal matter (*prakṛti*) and the evolutes of matter.

The grammatical subject of verses 2.5 to 2.9 is the self (*ātman*). Because this word is masculine, it would be grammatically correct to use the pronoun "he" rather than it. Such a translation would emphasize the personal aspect of the self (also here called "Great Lord"). Translating with the neuter pronoun "it," as I have done, emphasizes the abstract, philosophical aspect of *ātman* as identified with the ultimate reality, Brahman.

"Revealed texts" (*śruti*) refers specifically to the Vedas, the highest scriptural authority for most Hindus.

2.6 "Magician" (*māyin*) literally means "one who possesses magical power (*māyā*)." It is used frequently in the Īśvara Gītā as an epithet for Śiva (see 2.6, 2.27, 2.45, 3.22, 4.18, and 5.27).

"Magical power" (*māyā*) is sometimes translated as "illusion." More often in Sanskrit texts, however, this word is refers to the power of god or of *brahman* to create a phenomenal world that is taken by the ignorant to be the highest reality.

2.7 Verses 2.7 to 2.9 attempt to teach the nature of the highest self by the *via negativa*, by saying what it is not. This is most famously expressed in the Upaniṣads by the phrase "not this, not that" (*neti neti*).

2.8 This verse lists the five sense-objects, sound, touch, form, taste, and smell, and denies that the self is any of these things. These five sense-objects encompass all of our everyday objects of perception; by denying that the ultimate reality is any of these things, the poet denies that the ultimate reality is an object of perception.

"It is not the breath" appears to directly contradict 2.5, which says that "it is . . . the breath." However, because the word in question, *prāṇa,* has multiple meanings, commentators can read this section in a way that avoids contradiction. Besides it usual meaning of "breath," *prāṇa* also has secondary meanings of ultimate reality (*brahman*) and sense organs (*indriyas*). So, although in this verse the meaning may be breath, at 2.5 it may be understood as *brahman*. By reading texts such as the Īśvara Gītā in this way using secondary (*gauṇa*) meanings of words, commentators attempt to avoid what seem to be direct contradictions within the text.

2.9 This verse contains two extra quarters (sixteen extra syllables). This is not unusual for the epics and Purāṇas, whose language tends to be looser than some other types of Sanskrit poetic texts.

This verse again refers to concepts from Sāṃkhya philosophy: matter (*prakṛti*) and spirit (*puruṣa*) are the two separate ultimate principles of this dualistic philosophical system. However, according to some theistic forms of Sāṃkhya, both of these principles must be understood as creations of or aspects of god.

"Hands, feet, anus or genitals" refers directly to four of the five "organs of action" (*karmendriyas*) enumerated by Sāṃkhya philosophy. The fifth, speech, is mentioned in the previous verse. These organs of action are also parts of matter (*prakṛti*).

"In highest truth" translates *paramārthataḥ*. Some schools of Vedānta philosophy make a distinction between "highest truth" (*paramārtha-satya*) and "conventional truth" (*vyāvahārika-satya*).

2.11 In this verse, the Sāṃkhya philosophical concept of spirit (*puruṣa*) is used synonymously with the Vedānta concept of highest self (*paramātman*) at 2.10.

2.13 This explains how it is known that the self is not impure, infirm, or changeable (2.12). By means of yogic perception (*yogipratyakṣa*), sages are able to "see" their selves as they truly are. Because the self is not an object of ordinary perception (see 2.8), it is only available to this higher way of knowing.

2.15 Ordinarily, the word *bhoktṛ* means "enjoyer," the one who experiences states such as suffering and happiness. However, 2.14 says that the self is *not* the one who suffers. Here *bhoktṛ* may be understood as a synonym for "witness" (*sākṣin*), simply a disinterested observer of mental states.

2.18 This theme is reminiscent of one of the teachings of the Bhagavad Gītā: individual human beings are merely the instruments of a larger cosmic system as part of *prakṛti*; they themselves are not the true agents of action. Also see the note at 1.34.

2.22 This chapter insists repeatedly that in its "own nature" (*svabhāva*), the ultimate reality is one. It appears as many only due to "limiting conditions" (*upādhis*) that are not essential to the ultimate reality itself. On "limiting conditions," see note at 2.28.

2.26 Those who "see the physical as its essence" (*artha-svarūpam*) are materialists who deny the existence of the transcendent self, which is pure consciousness. The Cārvāka school in ancient India held this materialist view.

2.28 This is the classic metaphor used to clarify the philosophical concept of the "limiting condition" (*upādhi*), mentioned in several other verses. Although the crystal is pure and without color, it reflects the color of a flower or a seed in its proximity. The limiting condition, in this case the red object, makes people mistakenly think it has color. The same applies to the self (*ātman*) or spirit (*puruṣa*). It is pure consciousness, free from passions and impurities. But its proximity to the material world (*prakṛti*), full of such impurities, makes it appear to possess the properties of *prakṛti*. The similar metaphor of the clear sky and smoke appears at 2.24.

2.29 The injunction that one should hear about (*śrotavya*) the self refers to the study of "that which is heard" (*śruti*), a common term for the four Vedas and their branches. The other class of authoritative text is called "that which is remembered" (*smṛti*), and includes the epics, the Purāṇas, and legal texts. This passage alludes to the Bṛhadāraṇyaka Upaniṣad's threefold formula of hearing (*śravaṇa*), contemplating (*manana*), and meditating on (*nididhyāsana*) the highest truths of the Vedas (Bṛhadāraṇyaka Upaniṣad 2.4.5).

2.32 This refers to the Sāṃkhya philosophical school's concept of "aloneness" (*kaivalya*). But instead of understanding the self as being separate, as most texts of the Sāṃkhya philosophical school do, this verse identifies that state of being alone with "becoming one with the highest" (*ekībhūtaḥ pareṇa*).

2.35 I translate *māyā* in this verse and elsewhere as "magical power." Often the word *māyā* refers to god's power to create a world that, although apparently real, is not the ultimate reality. At other times *māyā* refers not to god's creative power, but to the effect of such power: the conventional world created by god. That is the sense in which it is used here.

2.38 This may be the "great yoga" (*mahāyoga*) mentioned at verse 11.7.

2.37 This famous simile of the rivers merging into the ocean occurs at Chāndogya Upaniṣad 6.10.1.

2.39 Patañjali's Yoga Sūtras 1.43–44 say there are two types of mental concentration (*samādhi*): concentration with concepts (*savikalpaka-samādhi*) and the higher stage of concentration without concepts (*nirvikalpaka-samādhi*) (see Bryant 2002:144–9). The Īśvara Gītā says that strictly speaking, knowledge accompanied by concepts is also ignorance (*ajñāna*).

2.40 For more on Yoga as "one pointed mental focus" (*ekacittatā*), see Īśvara Gītā 11.12.

2.42 The third foot of this verse is identical to Bhagavad Gītā 5.5. Just as in the Bhagavad Gītā, in most instances the Īśvara Gītā does not use the words *sāṃkhya* and *yoga* to refer to two different but related philosophical schools, as scholars often use the two words today. Instead, *sāṃkhya* corresponds roughly to "the path of knowledge," whereas yoga corresponds to "the path of mental concentration."

2.43 "Lordly powers" (*aiśvaryas*) here refer to the sorts of supernatural attainments described in Patañjali's Yoga Sūtras 3.16–48: for instance, becoming very large or very small, levitating, or inhabiting other beings' bodies. Some yogis become so caught up in the acquisition and use of these supernatural powers for their own selfish ends that they lose sight of the ultimate goal of liberation, conceived by the Īśvara Gītā as union with god.

2.44 In contrast to the ignorant magician-yogis described in the previous verse, wise people who have mastered both yoga and knowledge attain the true state of lordliness (*aiśvarya*), which is becoming Lord Śiva.

2.49 Alternatively: "Sages who see subtle things/ know that supreme lordliness/ is the cause of a self that is/ free from qualities and without stain." If this reading is accepted, then lordliness is strictly speaking the cause of *knowledge* of the self. It is not the cause of the self *per se*, because the self (*ātman*) is eternal and uncaused.

2.50 The third and fourth quarters of this verse are identical to the first and second quarters of Īśvara Gītā 4.1.

2.51 This theme, that Śiva delegates authority and is not involved directly in the world's governance, is emphasized throughout the Īśvara Gītā.

2.53 Although the word *nirvāṇa,* "extinguishing," was made famous by the Buddhists, it is also frequently used in the Purāṇas and other Hindu texts as a synonym for *mokṣa*, liberation from the cycle of death and rebirth. Also see note at 10.11.

2.54 The first quarter of this verse echoes Bṛhadāraṇyaka Upaniṣad 6.2.15.

A "cosmic cycle" (*kalpa*) equals 4,320,000,000 human years. For more on Purāṇic conceptions of time, see notes at 6.40 and 7.10.

A major question among Hindu theological traditions is whether one can achieve liberation by one's own effort alone, or whether the grace (*prasāda*) of god is required.

2.55 The idea that teachings of *sāṃkhya* (the path of knowledge) and *yoga* (the path of self-cultivation) should be given only to a restricted few appears throughout the Upaniṣads and Gītās. See, for example, Śvetāśvatara Upaniṣad 6.22, Bṛhadāraṇyaka Upaniṣad 6.3.12, Maitrī Upaniṣad 6.29, and Bhagavad Gītā 18.67.

It is unclear whether the reference to "sons" here should be understood in the sense of "sons and daughters" (the word *putra* can be used to mean "offspring" in general).

Chapter 3

3.1 "The unimanifest" (*avyakta*) here refers to *brahman,* as it also does at 3.3.

This chapter borrows heavily from the cosmology of the Sāṃkhya school of philosophy. However, it differs from the "classical" Sāṃkhya of the Sāṃkhya Kārikā, because it introduces the concepts of time (*kāla*) and *brahman,* which are not among the twenty-five principles (*tattvas*) mentioned in that text. For more on Sāṃkhya, see King (1999:166–89).

3.4 This verse uses technical terms from Indian epistemology. The "means of knowledge" (*pramāṇas*) are the tools that philosophers use to establish truth and validity. Examples of the *pramāṇas* include perception (*pratyakṣa*), rational inference (*anumāna*), scriptural authority (*śabdapramāṇa*), and comparison (*upamāna*). Because *brahman* is unique, it has no object of comparison (*upamāna*). The means of knowledge are not available to understand it as they are for worldly things. For more on epistemology in ancient India, see King (1999:128–46).

Mental construction (*vikalpa*) and semblance (*ābhāsa*) are also important philosophical concepts, discussed in Yoga, Vedānta, and Buddhist philosophies.

3.5 *Brahman* is space (*vyoma* or *ākāśa*) in a metaphorical sense. Like space, it is all-pervading and free from impurity (also see 2.24, 3.21).

3.6 The third and fourth quarters of this verse are identical to Īśvara Gītā 3.20.

3.8 In Sāṃkhya philosophy, the two fundamental principles (*tattvas*) are primeval matter (*prakṛti* or *pradhāna*) and spirit (*puruṣa*). Many Sāṃkhya texts say that the attraction between these two principles is automatic, like the attraction between iron filings and a magnet. However, other texts describe some external force beyond these two who bring them together at the beginning of each cosmic cycle. One possibility is that god unites these two principles. Another possibility, described here, is that time (*kāla*) brings the two together.

3.9 "These three" are time (*kāla*), primeval matter (*pradhāna*), and spirit (*puruṣa*), as described at 3.1 and 3.8. They exist in a relation of "difference-in-identity" (*bhedābheda*) with *brahman*, according to this verse. From one perspective they are the distinct entities; when analyzed in terms of *brahman* they are one.

3.10 This is a reference to Sāṃkhya cosmology, according to which there are twenty-three evolutes that issue from matter (*prakṛti*). The first of these is the intellect (*buddhi*), also known as "the great one" (*mahat*). The final evolutes are the five gross physical elements: space, air, fire, water, and earth. For more discussion and a chart of the evolutes, see King (1999:170–89).

The "deceiver" (*mohinī*) is an allusion to the myth from the Mahābhārata and the Purāṇas in which the god Viṣṇu incarnates as the seductress Mohinī in order to trick the demons into giving up the nectar of immortality. The name Mohinī comes from the verbal root *muh*, "to be confused." Like the beguiling female form of Viṣṇu, *prakṛti* seduces *puruṣa*. She confuses him and makes him forget that in reality he is entirely apart from the world of primal matter and its evolutes.

3.11 On the *guṇas* in Sāṃkhya philosophy, see note at 2.4.

Ego (*ahaṃkāra*) is the second evolute. It comes out of the intellect (*buddhi*) after the intellect has come out of *prakṛti*. It is responsible for creating the false understanding of selfhood. Besides *prakṛti* and its twenty-three evolutes, there is also spirit (*puruṣa*), which is in reality independent of *prakṛti*. It is therefore called the twenty-fifth principle (*tattva*).

3.12 The first evolute of *prakṛti* is called "the great one" (*mahat*) or "intellect" (*buddhi*) in the Sāṃkhya philosophy. Although intellect is not the true self (*ātman*), it is falsely identified as the self by those who are deluded by *prakṛti*. It makes determinate knowledge (*vijñāna*) possible, and is in that sense the knower (*vijñātṛ*).

3.13 The ego (*ahaṃkāra*) evolves from "the great one." Therefore, from one perspective, ego is not different from it.

3.14 Mind (*manas*) is the name of another evolute in the Sāṃkhya system, arising out of the ego (*ahaṃkāra*). It should not be confused with the intellect. It is lower than the intellect and ego, and it directly apprehends mental objects (such as feelings, thoughts, and memories). It is also responsible for assimilating the sense impressions created by the five sense organs.

3.15 Īśvara Gītā 3.8 describes time (*kāla*) as responsible for uniting the principles of matter (*prakṛti*) and spirit (*puruṣa*). Discriminative knowledge (*viveka*) of the two principles is what enables liberation, according to Sāṃkhya. According to this, it is time that is responsible for the lack of discriminative knowledge, since it joins the two principles.

3.17 Here and at 3.19, the author appears to apotheosize the breath (*prāṇa*) as "Lord Breath" (*bhagavān prāna*). Similarly Lord Agni, the god of fire, is mentioned at 3.20.

3.18 This is once again a reference to Sāṃkhya cosmology: intellect (*buddhi* or *mahat*) causes ego (*ahaṃkāra*), which in turn creates the mind (*manas*) and sense organs (*indriyas*).

3.19 By "the unmanifest" (*avyakta*) this verse means unmanifest matter (*prakṛti*), not unmanifest *brahman*. For atheistic Sāṃkhya, *puruṣa* is the highest principle. However, according to theistic Sāṃkhya texts such as the Īśvara Gītā, the lord (*īśvara* or *bhagavān*) controls *prakṛti* and *puruṣa*. Also see 6.8.

3.20 The third and fourth quarters of this verse are identical to Īśvara Gītā 3.6.

3.21 Space (*vyoma*) is sometimes translated as "ether." It is the subtlest of the five elements. It often is compared to god or *brahman*, as it is all-pervading and eternally pure. Also see note at 3.5.

3.22 On "magician" (*māyin*) and "magical power" (*māyā*), see notes at 2.6, 2.35.

Chapter 4

4.1 The first and second quarters of this verse are identical to the third and fourth quarters of Īśvara Gītā 2.50.

4.4 "The founder, provider, and the fire at the end of time" is an allusion to Śiva's three aspects: creator (Brahmā), preserver (Nārāyaṇa), and destroyer (Rudra). Also see 4.21–3.

4.9 "One who speaks of the Veda" translates *vedavādin*. Compare the similar word *brahmavādin* (note at 1.23).

4.10–11 In these two verses the author alludes to the four classes (*varṇas*). "Brahmins, warriors, and merchants" refers to the three twice-born *varṇas* in the Hindu class system. The fourth and lowest *varṇa*, servants (*śūdras*), also can be saved if they have devotion. "Those of low birth" (*nīcajātayaḥ*) refers both to śūdras and to outcastes, those who are born entirely outside the system of the four *varṇas*. According to Hindu legal texts, one's occupation is determined by the specific class (*varṇa*) and caste (*jāti*) that one is born into.

4.15 Here the god Brahmā, not the impersonal creative principle *brahman*, is meant.

4.18–19 On "magical power" and "magician," see notes at 2.6 and 2.35.

4.20 "Reservoir of immortality" (*nidhānam amṛtasya*) refers to the nectar of immortality churned out of the ocean by the gods (*devas*) and demons (*asuras*), one of part of the story of Viṣṇu's tortoise (*kūrma*) avatar.

4.21–3 These verses recapitulate the well known formulation of the "trio" (*trimūrti*) of gods from a Śaiva point of view. The three main gods Brahmā (the creator), Nārāyaṇa (the preserver), and Rudra (the destroyer) are all described as "powers" (*śaktis*) of Śiva, who is the highest god.

4.23 "Made up of darkness" (*tāmasī*) refers to one of the Sāṃkhya philosophical system's three *guṇas*, namely darkness or lethargy (*tamas*). For more on the three *guṇas*, see note at 2.4.

4.24 This verse lists the "four yogas," the four paths to god employed by people based on their different inclinations. These are the yoga of meditation (*dhyāna-yoga*), the yoga of knowledge (*jñāna-yoga*), the yoga of devotion (*bhakti-yoga*), and the yoga of action (*karma-yoga*). Swami Vivekananda, who knew the Īśvara Gītā, may have been inspired by this verse to create his own list of four yogas.

4.28 Strictly speaking, Śiva is pure eternal consciousness, and never performs any act—hence he is not the "director" (*prerayitṛ*). However, it is due to his mere existence that the entire world comes into being.

4.29 On "the great yoga" (*mahāyoga*), see verse 11.7.

4.30 If yoga is the same as "magical power" (*māyā*), it follows that the "lord of yoga" (*yogeśvara*) is the magician mentioned elsewhere (see note at 2.6).

4.31 "Principles" (*tattvas*) refers to the twenty-five principles of the Sāṃkhya philosophical school. See notes at 3.11, 3.14, and 7.22.

4.32 On "conceptual constructions" (*vikalpas*), see note at 2.39.

4.33 Śiva's cosmic dance, mentioned here, is manifested to the sages in chapter 5.

Chapter 5

5.1 This chapter is reminiscent of chapter 11 of the Bhagavad Gītā. There and here, human beings are granted divine vision to see the supreme form of god. The difference, of course, is that here Śiva is the supreme god, and the chapter portrays his famous Tāṇḍava dance of the creation, preservation, and destruction of the universe.

5.4 On "magical power" (*māyā*), see notes at 2.6 and 2.35.

5.9 The three radiant gods Sūrya (the sun), Soma (the moon), and Agni (fire) are described here as the three eyes of Lord Śiva.

5.11 This verse contains two extra quarters (of eight syllables each). See note at 2.10.

5.13 Although the literal expression here is "the time of time" (*kāla-kāla*), I have taken the second word in this compound in its sense of "destroyer"—to translate this word literally into English would render it incomprehensible. The Sanskrit world *kāla* is often figuratively used to refer to death (*mṛtyu*) or to Yama, the god of death.

5.17–20 These verses portay Harihara, the form of god that is Viṣṇu (Hari) and Śiva (Hara) combined: Viṣṇu on the left, Śiva on the right (verse 5.20). The Īśvara Gītā interprets this form by saying that Nārāyaṇa/Viṣṇu, is none other than Śiva when

Śiva is seen correctly in his highest lordly form. Elsewhere Nārāyaṇa is described as the power (*śakti*) of Śiva responsible for the world's preservation (see 4.22). Śiva also contains within himself the gods Sūrya, Soma, and Agni as his three eyes (see 5.9).

5.19–41 These verses employ the *triṣṭubh,* a different meter than used previously in this text. Most of the Īśvara Gītā is written in *anuṣṭubh,* four quarters of eight syllables each per verse. The *triṣṭubh* has four quarters of eleven syllables each per verse. The switch from *anuṣṭubh* to *triṣṭubh* to is sometimes used to emphasize or set apart the *triṣṭubh* verses. One example of this is in Bhagavad Gītā 11.15–50, where Kṛṣṇa reveals his highest, awe-inspiring form to Arjuna.

5.22 Here and at 5.25, I translate *puruṣa* as "person" rather than "spirit." The *puruṣa* in these passages appears to refer not to the Sāṃkhya dyad of *prakṛti* and *puruṣa,* but rather to the creator god, Brahmā. Brahmā was created by Lord Śiva and responsible for creating the world. He is also called Hiraṇyagarbha, the "golden egg," as the Purāṇas say he was born out of such an egg. Brahmā is described at 4.21 as the power (*śakti*) of Śiva responsible for the world's creation.

5.31 The word *śākha* means both a "branch" and, in the context of the Vedas, a lineage of oral transmission.

Although a frequent theme of the Īśvara Gītā is the all-inclusive form of Lord Śiva, verses like this seem to offer a more exclusivist message. The form of the Lord is one, and he is known through the Veda. Those who take refuge in him have peace, a peace that is not available to those who do not take refuge in him.

5.34 This and some of the other verses in this section call to mind the famous hymn at 1.64.46 of the Ṛg Veda: "They call him Indra, Mitra, Varuṇa, and Agni. He is the divine winged Garuḍa. He is one; sages call him by many names. They say he is Agni, Yama, and Mātariśvan."

5.37 This verse uses terms from some of the various philosophical schools: Vedāntins call the ultimate reality *brahman,* while according to this text, the Buddhists use the concept of the "empty" (*śūnya*) to refer to the same thing. On emptiness and the school of Madhyamaka Buddhist philosophy, see King (1999:119–27).

5.44 Earlier in chapter 5, Śiva revealed himself in his highest form, which encompasses Brahmā (the creator), Nārāyaṇa (the preserver), and Rudra (the destroyer). However, in his everyday form as Bhava, Lord Śiva appears as distinct from the other gods, hence Nārāyaṇa now once again stands beside him.

5.45 On "grace" (*prasāda*), see notes at 1.31 and 2.54.

5.47 "One who grants success in yoga" (*yoga-siddhidaḥ*) could also mean "one who grants yogic powers."

Chapter 6

6.4 "Simulacrum" (*upamā*) might also be translated as "comparison" or "resemblance." This word is used by Sanskrit literary theorists in a different context to mean "simile."

On "magical power" (*māyā*), see notes at 2.6 and 2.35.

6.5 Philosophers in India make a distinction between "power of action" (*kriyā-śakti*) and "power of thought" (*dhī-śakti*), the mental faculty.

6.8 This verse nicely encapsulates the role of god in Purāṇic Sāṃkhya. Rather than spirit (*puruṣa*) and matter (*prakṛti*) activating automatically as in the "classical" Sāṃkhya of the Sāṃkhya Kārikās, it is god who agitates them at the beginning of creation, setting them in motion. Also see Īśvara Gītā 3.19.

6.9 The "intellect" is the Sāṃkhya principle of *mahat* or *buddhi*, which is created out of *prakṛti*, and from which the other twenty-two principles of *prakṛti* are created. Also see Īśvara Gītā 3.18.

6.17 According to classical Indian medical thought, digestion occurs when food is burnt up by the body's internal fire. Agni, the god of fire, is "universal" (*vaiśvānara*) because he is the fire inside of all living beings.

6.19 According to classical Indian physiology, wind or vital energy (*prāṇa*) circulates throughout the body and is responsible for various functions. Often five different types of *prāṇa* are mentioned, each one with a specific purpose. Breath control (*prāṇayāma*) is important in premodern yoga as it is through mastery of breath control that the yogi controls the body's natural circulatory system. Wind is also apotheosized as "Lord Breath" (*bhagavān prāṇa*) at verse 3.17. For more on *prāṇayāma*, see the discussion in Bryant (2009:372–3).

6.25 Although Nirṛti is often portrayed as a feminine deity, the wife of Adharma (the god of anti-*dharma*), here Nirṛti is a masculine deity who bestows negative results of dark or wicked (*tāmasa*) acts (referring to *tamas*, one of the three *guṇas* of Sāṃkhya philosophy; see note at 2.4). Compare this to the portrayal of Śakra (Indra) at 6.22, who bestows positive results of Vedic sacrifice.

6.36 The god of fire is the "eternal destroyer" because it is he who burns up the entire world at the end of each world-cycle.

6.39 All of the beings described here are supernatural beings inferior to the gods (*devas*). I translate *yakṣas* as "spirits." They are attendants of the god of wealth Kubera, and usually not considered to be malevolent. "Demons" here refer to *rākṣasas*, blood-drinking malevolent beings such as Rāvaṇa, the god Rāma's foe in the Rāmāyaṇa. "Goblins" are *piśācas*, another class of flesh-eating beings.

6.40–4 These verses list the various divisions of time according to the Purāṇas, primarily based on the lunar calendar. Each lunar month (*māsa*) consists of two fortnights (*pakṣas*) of fourteen days each, one during the waxing and the other during the waning of the moon. There are six seasons (*ṛtus*) in one year.

The units of time listed at 6.40 deal with relatively short periods. A *kalā* is 1.6 minutes according to Laws of Manu 1.64; a *kāṣṭhā* is one-thirtieth of one *kalā*; a *muhūrta* is equivalent to forty-eight minutes (see Olivelle 2005:90–1).

Verse 6.41 deals with cosmological time. There are four *yugas*, of decreasing amounts: 1,728,000 years, 1,296,000 years, 864,000 years, and 432,000 years. Their sum total is one "great *yuga*" (*mahāyuga*). Seventy-one *mahāyugas* constitute an "age of Manu" (*manvantara*). Each age of Manu is equivalent to one-fourteenth of a day and night of the god Brahmā. A *para* is said to be the life span of the god Brahmā; a *parārdha* is half of Brahmā's life span.

6.42 The four classes of beings are those born from a womb (*jarayujya*); those born from an egg (*andaja*); those born from heat (*usmaja*); and those born from a seed (*udbhijja*).

6.43 Each universe (*brahmāṇda*, literally "egg of Brahmā") consists of seven hells and seven upper regions. There are innumerable universes according to the cosmology of the Purāṇas.

6.46 Primal matter (*prakṛti*) is the first principle in Sāṃkhya philosophy, from which other parts of nature evolve. See notes at 1.24, 2.5, and 2.9.

6.47 On the "deceiver" (*mohinī*), see note at 3.10.

At 3.10 it is matter (*prakṛti*), not magical power (*māyā*) that is described as the "deceiver of all embodied beings." Often these two words are used as synonyms in the Purāṇas and in medieval Vedānta. Both traditions borrow heavily from Sāṃkhya philosophy. Both the words *prakṛti* and *māyā* are feminine in gender.

6.48 Here the Vedānta term self (*ātman*) is identified with the Sāṃkhya principle of "spirit" (*puruṣa*).

Chapter 7

7.3–16 In these verses, Lord Śiva speaks of classes of beings, and describes himself as the best or highest of the beings in each of these classes. This is a common feature of many texts labeled in Sanskrit as "songs" (*gītās*). Compare, for instance, Bhagavad Gītā 10.21–39.

7.4 Śambhu is a name for Śiva in his benevolent form; the mountain king's daughter is the goddess Pārvatī, Śiva's consort. Ādityas and Vasus are different classes of deities. Both Ādityas and Vasus are deities associated with the sun.

7.6 By "the immortals' foes" (*amaradviṣ*), the text means the *asuras*, a class of ancient beings who fought the *devas* and are sometimes translated in English as "titans" or "demons." Strictly speaking, Prahlāda was not an enemy of the gods. According to the accounts of his story in the Purāṇas, he was an *asura* devoted to Viṣṇu who opposed his wicked father and sister.

7.9 As described in most Indian legal texts (*dharmaśāstras*), there are four stages of life: 1. Celibate student, 2. Householder, 3.

Forest-dweller, and 4. Renouncer. It is remarkable that here the householder stage is extolled as highest, since elsewhere the Īśvara Gītā extolls the life of the renouncer, or even suggests that it is possible to transcend the four *āśramas* entirely (see note at 11.67).

7.10 A *kalpa* can be a generic word for a span of time. It also can be a duration of time measuring 4,320,000,000 human years, one day in the life of Brahmā. A "great *kalpa*" (*mahākalpa*) is equivalent to the lifespan of Brahmā, 311,040,000,000,000 human years.

There are four *yugas*: the *kṛta, treta, dvāpara,* and *kali.* Each *yuga* is superior to the one that precedes it. Our current *yuga,* the *kaliyuga,* is characterized by discord, immorality, and short life spans among human beings. For the length of each of the four *yugas,* see note to 6.40–41.

The "god of wealth" is Kubera, king of the supernatural beings called *yakṣas*.

Vīraka is another name for Nandin, one of the most important leaders of Śiva's troops (*gaṇas*). Although in later times "Nandin" became the standard name for Śiva's vehicle, the bull (*ṛṣabha*), early Śaiva texts sometimes depicted Nandin as a powerful warrior with a monkey's face and a human body.

7.12 The Śatarudrīya is a hymn in the Yajur Veda praising the hundred forms of the god Rudra. It is also mentioned at 11.22 and 11.100.

7.13 The "hymn to the first man" is the famous Ṛg Veda section called the Puruṣa Sūkta, which describes how the entire world was created from the sacrifice of a giant man.

7.14 The "land of *brahman*" (*brahmāvarta*) is described at Laws of Manu 2.17 as the region between the Sarasvatī and Dṛṣadvatī rivers. This word might also be translated "Land of the Vedas."

7.18 This verse begins a new theme in chapter 7, the exposition of the theology of the Pāśupata sect (see introduction). The designation Pāśupatas give to the individual self is "beast" (*paśu*). Lord Śiva is the "master of beasts," Paśupati.

7.19 Here the important Hindu theological concept of God's play (*līlā*) is introduced. God creates the world not from any need or compulsion, but solely as a spontaneous act of joyful creativity. Although this concept is not mentioned in the Pāśupata Sūtras, it is prominent in later theistic philosophers such as Rāmānuja (see King 1999:228).

"One who speaks of the Veda" translates *vedavādin*. Compare the similar word *brahmavādin* (note at 1.23.)

7.22 This is another reference to the principles (*tattvas*) of the Sāṃkhya school of philosophy. The first eight principles created from primordial matter are termed "productive principles" (*prakṛtis*) because they, while being created, create something else in turn. The other fifteen "created principles" (*vikāras*) are created by the *prakṛtis*, but create nothing themselves. Note that although *prakṛti* often refers to the primordial matter (*mūlaprakṛti*) from which the twenty-three other created principles come, it can also be used in this wider sense. Also note that mind (*manas*), listed here as a productive principle (*prakṛti*), is generally considered to be a created principle (*vikāra*) in other Sāṃkhya texts. That is why other texts normally list sixteen created principles instead of fifteen (see Larson and Bhattacharya 1989: 48–53).

7.23–24 These verses continue with a list of the remaining fifteen of the twenty-three principles that evolve out of primordial matter (*mūlaprakṛti*). They include the five organs of sense (*buddhīndriyas*), the five organs of action (*karmendriyas*), and the five subtle elements (*tanmātras*). For more on the Sāṃkhya principles, see Larson and Bhattacharya (1987:48–53).

7.25 Although in atheistic Sāṃkhya *prakṛti* is by itself the cause of the entire world, in theistic Sāṃkhya texts such as this one it is understood as only the material cause that God uses to make the world, similar to the clay that a potter uses to make a pot.

7.26 On the three *guṇas*, see note at 2.4.

7.27 For Sāṃkhya, the cause of the "imbalance" (*vaiṣamya*) of the three *guṇas* is the "imbalance" or "error" (*vaiṣamya*) in the intellect that regards the self or spirit (*puruṣa*) as not something separate from the body, mind, and material elements.

7.28 *Dharma* and *adharma* here refer to righteous and unrighteous actions. Both are fetters insofar as both bind people to the cycle of death and rebirth. Even virtuous actions lead to rebirth, as they generate new, positive karmic results. However, by dedicating the fruits of one's actions to god without having and desire for those fruits, liberation can be attained while leading an active life. This is the teaching most closely associated with the Bhagavad Gītā, and is echoed in a few parts of the Īśvara Gītā (also see verses 11.80–84).

7.30 This verse asserts that magical power (*māyā*) is synonymous with original matter (*mūlaprakṛti*), and that both are a power (*śakti*) of God.

7.32 Here the meter switches from *anuṣṭubh* to *triṣṭubh* for just one verse (see note at 5.19).

On "spirit," see note at 1.24.

Chapter 8

8.4 This is another reference to the twenty five principles (*tattvas*) of Sāṃkhya philosophy. See notes at 3.11, 3.14, and 7.22.

8.8 On "magical power" (*māyā*), see notes at 2.6 and 2.35.

8.9 "Of all sciences" (*sarvavidyānāṃ*) refers to "sciences" in the wider sense, including disciplines such as poetics, astrology, statecraft, etc. It does not refer exclusively to the natural and social sciences, as the term is often used in English.

8.12 "Knowing the use of primal matter" (*pradhānaviniyogajñaḥ*) also can be translated, "knowing the disjunction of primal matter," that is, how to separate spirit (*puruṣa*) from matter (*prakṛti*). In Sāṃkhya philosophy, matter exists for the sake of spirit. By using matter skillfully (training one's mind and body), one achieves freedom from matter.

On the Sāṃkhya concepts of spirit and matter, see note at 1.24.

8.17 "Some call him one,/ others call him many" might be seen as a theological statement of difference-in-identity: god is both one and many. A similar statement comes at 10.8. A strict Advaita (monistic) reading of this text, however, would assert that only oneness is real. Manyness is an illusion caused by god's magical power of deception (*māyā*).

Chapter 9

9.1 The issue taken up here is that Śiva has said previously that the whole world is his form (*rūpa*). But the world appears to have very different characteristics than god. God is pure, eternal, and indivisible; the world is full of suffering, is subject to change, and has many different parts. Verses such as this show that the Īśvara Gītā's understanding of god's relation to the world is better described as *panentheism* than pantheism. The world is a part of him, yet he transcends it.

9.2 Although the creation of the world could not occur without god or *brahman*, he/it is not directly responsible for its creation. Instead, *māyā* is the world's material cause. This accounts for impurity and suffering in the world. Since God is free from all impurities and suffering, if there the world were identical to God, such things could not exist.

9.6 The meaning of the second half of this verse is obscure. I am taking it to mean that by means of just one magical power (*māyā*), an individual can find liberation and union with god. Māyā can itself be divided into parts, corresponding to different people, much as the Sāṃkhya system describes parts of *prakṛti* corresponding to each individual *puruṣa*. It is by means of skillful engagement with *māyā* that the self is liberated. Because according to some schools of Vedānta the entire world is *māyā*, even study of the Vedas and purification of the mind through yoga are ways of using *māyā* for liberation.

9.9 "That which is without beginning, middle, or end" is god or *brahman*. By the union of that with ignorance (*avidyā*), bondage and suffering occur. Yet this union is only apparent, not real, because *brahman* is pure and free from any flaw, just as the sky is not stained by smoke (see verse 2.24).

9.11 This verse relies on a metaphor from weaving. The highest abode of Viṣṇu is the loom, on which the world is spun up and down (*prota*) and back and forth (*ota*).

9.18 This verse emphasizes the importance of knowing the one true god. It may seem to contrast with other statements extolling both Śiva and Viṣṇu (e.g., 11.115), but is not necessarily contradictory.

Chapter 10

10.1 Chapter 10 begins with a play on the word "mark" (*liṅga*). Unmanifest *brahman* is *aliṅga*, free from any mark or characteristic (elsewhere called *nirguṇa*). But at the same time, *brahman* is the *liṅga*, the famous symbol of Śiva worshipped in temples throughout India. The meaning of Śiva's *liṅga* is explored in more detail in chapter 11 (11.92–98).

10.2 This verse suggests that through yoga one can achieve liberation, along with supernormal powers (*siddhis*), while still embodied in this world. The question of whether or not "embodied liberation" (*jīvanmukti*) is possible was hotly debated among philosophers in India.

The word *nirvāṇa*, closely associated with Buddhism, is also used in verses 2.53 and 10.11.

10.5 On magical power (*māyā*), see notes at 2.6 and 2.35.

10.7 The question as to whether selves are one or many was debated by philosophical schools in India. The Advaita Vedānta school sees the individual self (*jīvātman*) to be one and identical to *brahman*. Other Vedānta schools, however, uphold the multiplicity of individual selves, arguing that if the self were one, then when one person becomes liberated, all people would become liberated. The "classical" Sāṃkhya of the Sāṃkhya Kārikās also argued for the existence of many distinct "spirits" (*puruṣas*). The Īśvara Gītā seems to suggest here that exponents of either philosophical position can achieve liberation. For more on these different philosophies, see King (1999:166–89, 212–29).

10.8 Here allowance is made for the worship the many different gods because they are all ultimately the same as *brahman*, the ultimate reality. Through devotion to just one god or aspect of *brahman*, the worshipper eventually knows the totality of *brahman*. On the idea that god is both one and many, also see note at 8.17.

10.11 In this verse, the goals of several different spiritual paths are all identified as the same: The union with god that is the goal of theistic sects, the *nirvāṇa* of the Buddhists, the oneness with *brahman* of Vedānta, and the aloneness (*kaivalya*) of Sāṃkhya. Also see note at 2.53.

Chapter 11

11.2 The "cage of evils" is *saṃsāra,* the cycle of death and rebirth. Yogis who have achieved the state of embodied liberation (*jīvanmukti*) are no longer subject to the bondage and suffering of *saṃsāra.*

I take *siddhi* here to refer specifically to the extraordinary powers one attains as a part of the yogic path. These powers are described in the third chapter of Patañjali's Yoga Sūtras. The second half of this verse could also be translated "Pure knowledge arises, leading directly to the attainment of *nirvāṇa.*" Also see note at 11.56.

11.4 Those who take Śiva as their meditative object become Śiva himself. The epithet "Great Lord" (*māheśvara*) is commonly applied to the god Śiva. But "Lord" (*īśvara*) or "Great Lord" (*māheśvara*) is also used to refer to advanced yoga practitioners who partake of the lord's power (*aiśvarya*). Also see 2.43, 2.44, 2.49.

11.6 Although the "yoga of non-being" (*abhāvayoga*) is useful for helping the practitioner distinguish the real self from false appearances, it fails to illuminate the relation of the self and universe to god (understood here to be Lord Śiva). The "yoga of non-being" described here has similarities to the one mentioned in the Śiva Purāṇa (7.2.37.7–10) and Liṅga Purāṇa (2.55.14).

11.8 "The yoga of *brahman*" is the same as "the yoga on me" discussed at 11.4 (the "great yoga").

11.10 "Those who reject the lord" (*īśvarabahiṣkṛtāḥ*) is more literally "those who expel the lord" or "those who drive out the lord." It may refer to atheistic yogis, or it may refer more generally to any yogi who does not see Śiva as the highest lord.

11.11–12 This list of the eight means (*sādhanas*) of *yoga* is identical to the list of the eight limbs (*aṅgas*) given in Patañjali's Yoga Sūtra 2.28, albeit in a different order. In subsequent verses, the Īśvara Gītā details each of the eight in the same order as the Yoga Sūtras, with one exception. The postures are explained last, after absorption (*samādhi*), the limb of *yoga* considered highest by Patañjali. (On Patañjali's eight limbs, see Bryant 2009:241.)

An important difference between the two texts is the Īśvara Gītā's theocentric definition of *yoga* as the focus of the mind exclusively on God through suppression of all other mental activity. Patañjali's defines *yoga* at Yoga Sūtra 1.2 simply as "suppression of mental activity" (*citta-vṛtti-nirodha*) without any mention of God. Patañjali does mention concentration on the Lord (*īśvara-praṇidhāna*) as one of the observances (*niyamas*) at Yoga Sūtra 1.23. But Īśvara is not clearly at the center of the Yoga Sūtras in the way that he is of the Īśvara Gītā, nor is it likely in the Yoga Sūtras that Patañjali uses the word *īśvara* to mean Lord Śiva, the creator, preserver, and destroyer of the world.

11.13 This list of restraints is identical to the one at Yoga Sūtra 2.30.

11.15 The author of the Īśvara Gītā offers a proviso regarding non-harming (*ahiṃsā*). Because the Vedas require certain animal sacrifices, these acts might seem to be prohibited by the principle of non-harming. This is not the case, as these violent acts too should considered falling under the text's definition of *ahiṃsā*. This is the position of the Mīmāṃsā school, which insists on the necessity in certain types of ritual violence that are prescribed by the Vedas. "Scripture's injunction" (*vidhi*) refers specifically to injunctions of the Vedas, not of any other texts. The most frequently cited example of this exception in cases of ritual violence is from the Laws of Manu (verse 5.44): "When a killing (*hiṃsā*) is sanctioned by the Veda and well-established in this mobile and immobile creation, it should be regarded definitely as a non-killing (*ahiṃsā*); for it is from the Veda that the Law has shined forth" (translated in Olivelle 2005:140).

Notably, this proviso does not appear in the Yoga Sūtras of Patañjali or its commentaries, which explicitly say that non-harming and the other restraints are universal, not subject to any exceptions (YS 2.31). In commenting on this sūtra by Patañjali, Vyāsa writes that those who believe that they will acquire merit from violent animal sacrifices are confused, and that they incur demerit instead. Kauṇḍinya's commentary on the Pāśupata Sūtras also rejects any exception to the universal rule of *ahiṃsā*. The proviso in this verse can be interpreted as the Īśvara Gītā's concession to mainstream views about the necessity of animal sacrifice. For more on *ahiṃsā* in Indian traditions, see Halbfass (1990:87–129).

11.19 This can also be translated as "not accepting possessions from desire (*yathecchayā*)." Most sects in India allow some possessions for a mendicant, such as a robe and begging bowl. But accepting gifts of food, for instance, should be disinterested and solely to nourish the body, not from any craving for the taste of the food.

11.20 This list of observances appears at Yoga Sūtra 2.32, with "concentration on the Lord" (*īśvara-praṇidhāna*) in the Yoga Sūtra replaced in the Īśvara Gītā with "worship of the Lord" (*īśvara-pūjana*).

11.21 The extended (*parāka*) fast is described at Laws of Manu 11.216: "When a man, controlled and vigilant, abstains from food for twelve days, it is called the *Parāka* penance, which removes all sins." The lunar (*cāndrāyaṇa*) penance is described in Manu 11.217: "He should decrease his food by one rice-ball a day during the dark fortnight and increase it likewise during the bright fortnight, bathing three times a day—tradition calls this *Cāndrāyaṇa* (the lunar penance)" (see Olivelle 2005: 226–7).

11.22 On the Śatarudrīya, see note at 7.12.

11.25 Compare this verse to Laws of Manu verses 2.85–87 (Olivelle 2005:99).

11.26 All three of these types of recitation—voiced, unvoiced, and mental—both involve repetition of the words of the text and comprehension of the words of the text. Mere repetition of the sounds of the words without comprehension, as is commonly practiced by worshippers who do not understand Sanskrit, is not Vedic study (*svādhyāya*).

11.28 Purification by earth (*mṛd*) refers to the smearing the body with ashes (*bhasma*) practiced by the Pāśupatas and other Śaiva sects. Also see 11.66.

11.29 According to this text, verbal worship is praise (*stuti*) of Śiva, mental worship is remembrance (*smṛti*) of Śiva, and physical worship, such as offering fruit or flowers to Śiva, is simply known as worship (*pūjana*).

11.32 The commentator Vijñānabhikṣu specifies that a "beat" (*mātrā*) is equivalent to the time it takes to say one short syllable.

11.34 Although the type of recitation (*japa*) that accompanies breath control exercises is not specified, from context it is clear that mental recitation is meant.

11.35 This is the author's instruction for breath control "with seed" (*sagarba*). The Gāyatrī mantra is a very well-known mantra from the Ṛg Veda. This verse says that it should always be preceded by its "head" (*śiras*), which consists of the syllable Oṃ and the words *bhūr bhūvaḥ svaḥ* (known as the *vyāhṛti*).

11.38 "Restraint of the sense organs" refers to the generally accepted theory of perception among philosophers in ancient India: The sense organs themselves move toward and come into contact with the objects of sense. This contact is the cause of the arising of the five types of sense perceptions. Although the sense organs of the undisciplined person automatically move toward and engage with sense objects, a disciplined yogi is able to stop the sense organs from extending out from the body toward their objects. For more on this projective theory of perception, see White (2009: 123–6)

11.43 The author departs from Patañjali's ordering of the eight limbs (*aṅgas*) of *yoga* by describing posture (*āsana*) after absorption (*samādhi*). This creates ambiguity about which of the Īśvara Gītā's eight means (*sādhanas*) should be considered highest. After stating at 11.41 that absorption is the highest means, at 11.43 the author states that posture is the highest. In light of the Īśvara Gītā's understanding of the highest yoga as union between the individual and Lord Śiva, the statement at 11.43 should probably be taken as hyperbole.

11.50–51 On the proper place for the performance of yoga, compare this verse with Śvetāśvatara Upaniṣad 2.10 and Bhagavad Gītā 6.11–12.

11.54 On "magical power" (*māyā*), see notes at 2.6 and 2.35.

11.56 The "lordly powers" (*aiśvaryas*) are supernatural abilities acquired in the course of the practice of yoga. Although they may be used toward positive ends, the Īśvara Gītā warns against focusing on these powers exclusively and losing sight of the end goal of yoga (see Īśvara Gītā 2.43).

The eight petals of the lotus may correspond to the eight *aiśvaryas* enumerated by yoga commentators. One common version of this list is: 1. becoming very small; 2. becoming very light; 3. Becoming very large; 4. The ability to attain anything; 5. Fulfillment of all desires; 6. Having complete control of other beings; 7. Being lord of the world; 8. Being able to manipulate the elements (see Bryant 2009:384–5).

11.61 "Spirit" is a translation of *puruṣa*, the twenty-fifth principle (*tattva*) of Sāṃkhya philosophy. It is pure and different separate from other twenty-four principles. According to Yoga Sūtra 1.24, the lord is himself a spirit who differs from all others on account of his never having been subject to impurity of any sort.

11.66 The mantra beginning with 'fire'" is in the Atharvaśiras Upaniṣad. It describes the Pāśupatas as smearing their bodies with ashes and reciting the mantra "Fire is ashes, wind is ashes, water is ashes, dry land is ashes, the sky is ashes. All this is ashes, the mind, these eyes are ashes" (Atharvaśiras Upaniṣad 39; see Tarkaratna 1990).

There are an extra two quarters, of eight syllables each, in this verse (see note at 2.10).

11.67 The Pāśupatas were one of the earliest recorded groups to be devoted to Śiva. It was they who composed most of the Īśvara Gītā. They taught that individual selves (*paśus,* "creatures") can be liberated from their fetters (*pāśas*) by means of identification with Lord Śiva (the *pati,* "master") using visualization exercises of the sort described from 11.53–66. Refer to the introduction for more information.

"Stages of life" refers to the four stages (*āśramas*) taught as obligatory in Hindu legal texts: student, householder, forest-dweller, and renouncer. The Pāśupatas maintained that their vow was a fifth stage beyond the four outlined in most legal texts. This is why the Pāśupata path is often described as the *atimarga,* "the path beyond [the four stages]" (see Sanderson 2005:158). Kauṇḍinya's commentary on the Pāśupata Sūtras suggests that only brahmin males who have already undergone the sacred thread (*upanayana*) ceremony are qualified to take Pāśupata vow, although in practice, other twice-borns may have been initiated as well (see introduction).

11.68 Here the nine limbs of another vow (*vratāṅgāni*) are described. Note that of these nine, non-harming, truthfulness, and celibacy were included among the restraints (*yamas*) at 11.13, and austerity, contentment, and purity were included among the observances (*niyamas*) at 11.20.

Affirmation (*āstikya*) literally means, "being one who says, 'there is.' " The precise nature of the affirmation varies according to different sources. Early uses of this term seem to have referred to "one who affirms the existence of an afterlife." In later times it came to be defined primarily as "one who affirms the authority of the Vedas" (see Nicholson 2010:168–84).

11.71 This verse begins a series of verses in chapter 11 that are borrowed in part or in whole from the Bhagavad Gītā. For some reflections on the relationship between the Īśvara Gītā and the Bhagavad Gītā, refer to the introduction. For a list of verses identical to those in Bhagavad Gītā and other texts, refer to the list of concordances.

11.74 Compare this verse to 11.81: This verse simply says "one who surrenders all actions," suggesting complete renunciation of all worldly acts. Verse 11.81 expands this as "one who surrenders all actions to me in his mind," repeating the Bhagavad Gītā's exhortation to act in accordance with legal texts while devoting the fruits of action to God (Bhagavad Gītā 18.57).

11.80 This verse begins a discourse on *karma-yoga,* the yoga of action. This theme of acting while renouncing the fruits of one's actions is much more common in the Bhagavad Gītā than the Īśvara Gītā. Like Patañjali's Yoga Sūtras, the Īśvara Gītā's main concern is the life of the renouncer (*saṃnyāsin*), not the householder (*gṛhastha*).

11.81 See note at 11.74.

11.92 Here again is the exhortation to abandon all worldly ties, including "sons and family," something not taught in the Bhagavad Gītā's exhortation to act without concern for the fruits of action. Additionally, worship of the *liṅga* is mentioned here, one of the central practices of Śaiva ascetics.

11.93 On achieving liberation and supernatural powers while still embodied, see note at 11.2.

11.98 This memorable verse is a reminder that the *liṅga* is not merely an object or a phallic symbol: It is an omnipresent reality and metaphysical principle.

11.100 On the Śatarudrīya, see note at 7.12.

11.111–115 Although these verses condemn those who would criticize Vaiṣṇavas, it also takes a typically Śaiva attitude toward Viṣṇu and other gods: Viṣṇu should be revered because he is a form of the highest god, Śiva.

11.117 "Dog-cooker" (*śvapāka*) is a pejorative term for a cāṇḍala, one of the lowest of all outcaste groups. In the eyes of Śiva, someone who reviles Nārāyaṇa is even worse than the lowest of the low, someone who cooks and eats dogs.

11.129 It is the sage Vyāsa who is speaking here, hence "my father Parāśara."

11.131 This is a reference to Kṛṣṇa's teaching to Arjuna in the Bhagavad Gītā.

11.134 According to this verse, the worship of Śiva is encouraged for the sages' wives.

11.135 "Benevolent" (Śaṅkara) is another name of Śiva.

11.137 Here resumes the narration by Sūta, pupil of Vyāsa. Vyāsa narrates from 1.15 to 11.136.

11.141 On the "tortoise" (*kūrma*) avatar of Viṣṇu, see note at 1.13.

11.142 This may refer to the Vyāsa Gītā (Song of Vyāsa), the excursus on *dharma* that follows the Īśvara Gītā in the Kūrma Purāṇa.

Sanskrit Text

Chapter 1

ṛṣaya ūcuḥ

1. bhavatā kathitaḥ samyak sargaḥ svāyaṃbhuvas tataḥ
brahmāṇḍasyāsya vistāro manvantaraviniścayaḥ
2. tatreśvareśvaro devo varṇibhir dharmatatparaiḥ
jñānayogaratair nityam ārādhyaḥ kathitas tvayā[1]
3. tadvadāśeṣasaṃsāraduḥkhanāśanam uttamam
jñānaṃ brahmaikaviṣayaṃ yena paśyema tat param[2]
4. tvaṃ hi nārāyaṇāt sākṣāt kṛṣṇadvaipāyanāt prabho
avāptākhilavijñānas tat tvāṃ pṛcchāmahe punaḥ
5. śrutvā munīnāṃ tad vākyaṃ kṛṣṇadvaipāyanaṃ prabhum
sūtaḥ paurāṇikaḥ smṛtvā bhāṣituṃ hy upacakrame
6. athāsminn antare vyāsaḥ kṛṣṇadvaipāyanaḥ svayam
ājagāma muniśreṣṭhā yatra satraṃ samāsate
7. taṃ dṛṣṭvā vedavidvāṃsaṃ kālameghasamadyutim
vyāsaṃ kamalapatrākṣaṃ praṇemur dvijapuṃgavāḥ
8. papāta daṇḍavad bhūmau dṛṣṭvāsau romaharṣaṇaḥ
pradakṣiṇīkṛtya guruṃ prāñjaliḥ pārśvago 'bhavat[3]
9. pṛṣṭāste 'nāmayaṃ viprāḥ śaunakādyā mahāmunim
samāśvāsyāsanaṃ tasmai tadyogyaṃ samakalpayan
10. athaitān abravīd vākyaṃ parāśarasutaḥ prabhuḥ
kaccin na tapaso hāniḥ svādhyāyasya śrutasya ca
11. tataḥ sa sūtaḥ svaguruṃ praṇamyāha mahāmunim
jñānaṃ tad brahmaviṣayaṃ munīnāṃ vaktum arhasi
12. ime hi munayaḥ śāntās tāpasā dharmatatparāḥ
śuśrūṣā jāyate caiṣāṃ vaktum arhasi tattvataḥ

13. jñānaṃ vimuktidaṃ divyaṃ yan me sākṣāt tvayoditam
munīnāṃ vyāhṛtaṃ pūrvaṃ viṣṇunā kūrmarūpiṇā

14. śrutvā sūtasya vacanaṃ muniḥ satyavatīsutaḥ
praṇamya śirasā rudraṃ vacaḥ prāha sukhāvaham

vyāsa uvāca

15. vakṣye devo mahādevaḥ pṛṣṭo yogīśvaraiḥ purā
sanatkumārapramukhaiḥ svayaṃ yat samabhāṣata

16. sanatkumāraḥ sanakas tathaiva ca sanandanaḥ
aṅgirā rudrasahito bhṛguḥ paramadharmavit

17. kaṇādaḥ kapilo yogī vāmadevo mahāmuniḥ
śukro vasiṣṭho bhagavān sarve saṃyatamānasāḥ

18. parasparaṃ vicāryaite saṃśayāviṣṭacetasaḥ
taptavantas tapo ghoraṃ puṇye badarikāśrame[4]

19. apaśyaṃs te mahāyogam ṛṣiṃ dharmasutaṃ śucim
nārāyaṇam anādyantaṃ nareṇa sahitaṃ tadā

20. saṃstūya vividhaiḥ stotraiḥ sarve vedasamudbhavaiḥ
praṇemur bhaktisaṃyuktā yogino yogavittamam

21. vijñāya vāñchitaṃ teṣāṃ bhagavān api sarvavit
prāha gambhīrayā vācā kim arthaṃ tapyate tapaḥ

22. abruvan hṛṣṭamanaso viśvātmānaṃ sanātanam
sākṣān nārāyaṇaṃ devam āgataṃ siddhisūcakam

23. vayaṃ saṃśayam āpannāḥ sarve vai brahmavādinaḥ
bhavantam ekaṃ śaraṇaṃ prapannāḥ puruṣottamam

24. tvaṃ hi tad vettha paramaṃ sarvajño bhagavān ṛṣiḥ
nārāyaṇaḥ svayaṃ sākṣāt purāṇo 'vyaktapūruṣaḥ

25. na hy anyo vidyate vettā tvām ṛte parameśvara
śuśrūṣāsmākam akhilaṃ saṃśayaṃ chettum arhasi

26. kiṃkāraṇam idaṃ kṛtsnaṃ ko 'nusaṃsarate sadā
kaścid ātmā ca kā muktiḥ saṃsāraḥ kiṃnimittakaḥ[5]

27. kaḥ saṃsārayatīśānaḥ ko vā sarvaṃ prapaśyati
kiṃ tat parataraṃ brahma sarvaṃ no vaktum arhasi

28. evam ukte tu munayaḥ prāpaśyan puruṣottamam
vihāya tāpasaṃ rūpaṃ saṃsthitaṃ svena tejasā

29. vibhrājamānaṃ vimalaṃ prabhāmaṇḍalamaṇḍitam
śrīvatsavakṣasaṃ devaṃ taptajāmbūnadaprabham

30. śaṅkhacakragadāpāṇiṃ śārṅgahastaṃ śriyāvṛtam
na dṛṣṭas tatkṣaṇād eva naras tasyaiva tejasā

31. tadantare mahādevaḥ śaśāṅkāṅkitaśekharaḥ
prasādābhimukho rudraḥ prādur āsīn maheśvaraḥ

32. nirīkṣya te jagannāthaṃ trinetraṃ candrabhūṣaṇam
tuṣṭuvur hṛṣṭamanaso bhaktyā taṃ parameśvaram

33. jayeśvara mahādeva jaya bhūtapate śiva
jayāśeṣamunīśāna tapasābhiprapūjita

34. sahasramūrte viśvātman jagadyantrapravartaka
jayānanta jagajjanmatrāṇasaṃhārakāraṇa

35. sahasracaraṇeśāna śaṃbho yogīndravandita
jayāmbikāpate deva namaste parameśvara

36. saṃstuto bhagavān īśas tryambako bhaktavatsalaḥ
samāliṅgya hṛṣīkeśaṃ prāha gambhīrayā girā

37. kimarthaṃ puṇḍarīkākṣa munīndrā brahmavādinaḥ
imaṃ samāgatā deśaṃ kiṃ vā kāryaṃ mayācyuta

38. ākarṇya bhagavadvākyaṃ devadevo janārdanaḥ
prāha devo mahādevaṃ prasādābhimukhaṃ sthitam[6]

39. ime hi munayo deva tāpasāḥ kṣīṇakalmaṣāḥ
abhyāgatā māṃ śaraṇaṃ samyagdarśanakāṅkṣiṇaḥ

40. yadi prasanno bhagavān munīnāṃ bhāvitātmanām
sannidhau mama taj jñānaṃ divyaṃ vaktum ihārhasi

41. tvaṃ hi vettha svam ātmānaṃ na hy anyo vidyate śiva
tatas tvam ātmanātmānaṃ munīndrebhyaḥ pradarśaya

42. evam uktvā hṛṣīkeśaḥ provāca munipuṅgavān
pradarśayan yogasiddhiṃ nirīkṣya vṛṣabhadhvajam

43. saṃdarśanān maheśasya śaṅkarasyātha śūlinaḥ
kṛtārthaṃ svayam ātmānaṃ jñātum arhatha tattvataḥ

44. praṣṭum arhatha viśveśaṃ pratyakṣaṃ purataḥ sthitam
mamaiva sannidhāv eṣa yathāvad vaktum īśvaraḥ

45. niśamya viṣṇuvacanaṃ praṇamya vṛṣabhadhvajam
sanatkumārapramukhāḥ pṛcchanti sma maheśvaram

46. athāsminn antare divyam āsanaṃ vimalaṃ śivam
kim apy acintyaṃ gaganād īśvarārhaṃ samudbabhau

47. tatrāsasāda yogātmā viṣṇunā saha viśvakṛt
tejasā pūrayan viśvaṃ bhāti devo maheśvaraḥ

48. taṃ te devādideveśaṃ śaṅkaraṃ brahmavādinaḥ
vibhrājamānaṃ vimale tasmin dadṛśur āsane

49. yaṃ prapaśyanti yogasthāḥ svātmany ātmānam īśvaram
ananyatejasaṃ śāntaṃ śivaṃ dadṛśire kila[7]

50. yataḥ prasūtir bhūtānāṃ yatraitat pravilīyate
tam āsanasthaṃ bhūtānām īśaṃ dadṛśire kila

51. yadantarā sarvam etad yato 'bhinnam idaṃ jagat
savāsudevam āsīnaṃ tam īśaṃ dadṛśuḥ kila[8]

52. provāca pṛṣṭo bhagavān munīnāṃ parameśvaraḥ
nirīkṣya puṇḍarīkākṣaṃ svātmayogam anuttamam

53. tac chṛṇudhvaṃ yathānyāyam ucyamānaṃ mayānaghāḥ
praśāntamānasāḥ sarve jñānam īśvarabhāṣitam

Chapter 2

īśvara uvāca

1. avācyam etad vijñānam ātmaguhyaṃ sanātanam
yan na devā vijānanti yatanto 'pi dvijātayaḥ

2. idaṃ jñānaṃ samāśritya brahmabhūtā dvijottamāḥ
na saṃsāraṃ prapadyante pūrve 'pi brahmavādinaḥ

3. guhyād guhyatamaṃ sākṣād gopanīyaṃ prayatnataḥ
vakṣye bhaktimatām adya yuṣmākaṃ brahmavādinām

4. ātmāyaḥ kevalaḥ svasthaḥ śāntaḥ sūkṣmaḥ sanātanaḥ
asti sarvāntaraḥ sākṣāc cinmātras tamasaḥ paraḥ

5. so 'ntaryāmī sa puruṣaḥ sa prāṇaḥ sa maheśvaraḥ
sa kālo 'gnis tad avyaktaṃ sa evedam iti śrutiḥ

6. asmād vijāyate viśvam atraiva pravilīyate
sa māyī māyayā baddhāḥ karoti vividhās tanūḥ[9]

7. na cāpy ayaṃ saṃsarati na ca saṃsārayet prabhuḥ
nāyaṃ pṛthvī na salilaṃ na tejaḥ pavano nabhaḥ

8. na prāṇo na mano 'vyaktaṃ na śabdaḥ sparśa eva ca
na rūparasagandhāś ca nāhaṃ kartā na vāg api

9. na pāṇipādau no pāyur na copasthaṃ dvijottamāḥ
na kartā na ca bhoktā vā na ca prakṛtipūruṣau
na māyā naiva ca prāṇaś caitanyaṃ paramārthataḥ

10. yathā prakāśatamasoḥ sambandho nopapadyate
tadvad aikyaṃ na saṃbandhaḥ prapañcaparamātmanoḥ

11. chāyātapau yathā loke parasparavilakṣaṇau
tadvat prapañcapuruṣau vibhinnau paramārthataḥ

12. yady ātmā malino 'svastho vikārī syāt svabhāvataḥ
na hi tasya bhaven muktir janmāntaraśatair api

13. paśyanti munayo yuktāḥ svātmānaṃ paramārthataḥ
vikārahīnaṃ nirduḥkham ānandātmānam avyayam

14. ahaṃ kartā sukhī duḥkhī kṛśaḥ sthūleti yā matiḥ
sā cāhaṃkārakartṛtvād ātmany āropyate janaiḥ

15. vadanti vedavidvāṃsaḥ sākṣiṇaṃ prakṛteḥ param
bhoktāram akṣaraṃ śuddhaṃ sarvatra samavasthitam

16. tasmād ajñānamūlo hi saṃsāraḥ sarvadehinām
ajñānād anyathājñānāt tattvaṃ prakṛtisaṃgatam[10]

17. nityoditaḥ svayaṃ jyotiḥ sarvagaḥ puruṣaḥ paraḥ
ahaṃkārāvivekena kartāham iti manyate

18. paśyanti ṛṣayo 'vyaktaṃ nityaṃ sadasadātmakam
pradhānaṃ prakṛtiṃ buddhvā kāraṇaṃ brahmavādinaḥ

19. tenāyaṃ saṃgato hy ātmā kūṭastho 'pi nirañjanaḥ
svātmānam akṣaraṃ brahma nāvabuddhyeta tattvataḥ

20. anātmany ātmavijñānaṃ tasmād duḥkhaṃ tathetaram
rāgadveṣādayo doṣāḥ sarve bhrāntinibandhanāḥ

21. karmaṇy asya bhaved doṣaḥ puṇyāpuṇyam iti sthitiḥ
tadvaśād eva sarveṣāṃ sarvadehasamudbhavaḥ

22. nityaḥ sarvatrago hy ātmā kūṭastho doṣavarjitaḥ
ekaḥ sa bhidyate śaktyā māyayā na svabhāvataḥ

23. tasmād advaitam evāhur munayaḥ paramārthataḥ
bhedo vyaktasvabhāvena sā ca māyātmasaṃśrayā

24. yathā hi dhūmasaṃparkān nākāśo malino bhavet
antaḥkaraṇajair bhāvair ātmā tadvan na lipyate

25. yathā svaprabhayā bhāti kevalaḥ sphaṭiko 'malaḥ
upādhihīno vimalas tathaivātmā prakāśate

26. jñānasvarūpam evāhur jagad etad vicakṣaṇāḥ
arthasvarūpam evājñāḥ paśyanty anye kudṛṣṭayaḥ

27. kūṭastho nirguṇo vyāpī caitanyātmā svabhāvataḥ
dṛśyate hy artharūpeṇa puruṣair bhrāntidṛṣṭibhiḥ

28. yathā saṃlakṣyate raktaḥ kevalaḥ sphaṭiko janaiḥ
raktikādyupadhānena tadvat paramapūruṣaḥ

29. tasmād ātmākṣaraḥ śuddho nityaḥ sarvagato 'vyayaḥ
upāsitavyo mantavyaḥ śrotavyaś ca mumukṣubhiḥ

30. yadā manasi caitanyaṃ bhāti sarvatragaṃ sadā
yogino 'vyavadhānena tadā saṃpadyate svayam

31, yadā sarvāṇi bhūtāni svātmany evābhipaśyati
sarvabhūteṣu cātmānaṃ brahma saṃpadyate tadā

32. yadā sarvāṇi bhūtāni samādhistho na paśyati
ekībhūtaḥ pareṇāsau tadā bhavati kevalaḥ

33. yadā sarve pramucyante kāmā ye 'sya hṛdi sthitāḥ
tadāsāv amṛtībhūtaḥ kṣemaṃ gacchati paṇḍitaḥ

34. yadā bhūtapṛthagbhāvam ekastham anupaśyati
tata eva ca vistāraṃ brahma saṃpadyate tadā

35. yadā paśyati cātmānaṃ kevalaṃ paramārthataḥ
māyāmātraṃ jagat kṛtsnaṃ tadā bhavati nirvṛtaḥ

36. yadā janmajarāduḥkhavyādhīnām ekabheṣajam
kevalaṃ brahmavijñānaṃ jāyate 'sau tadā śivaḥ

37. yathā nadīnadā loke sāgareṇaikatāṃ yayuḥ
tadvad ātmākṣareṇāsau niṣkalenaikatāṃ vrajet

38. tasmād vijñānam evāsti na prapañco na saṃsṛtiḥ
ajñānenāvṛtaṃ loko vijñānaṃ tena muhyati

39. taj jñānaṃ nirmalaṃ sūkṣmaṃ nirvikalpaṃ yad avyayam
ajñānam itarat sarvaṃ vijñānam iti me matam

40. etad vaḥ paramaṃ sāṃkhyaṃ bhāṣitaṃ jñānam uttamam
sarvavedāntasāraṃ hi yogas tatraikacittatā

41. yogāt saṃjāyate jñānaṃ jñānād yogaḥ pravartate
yogajñānābhiyuktasya nāvāpyaṃ vidyate kvacit

42. yad eva yogino yānti sāṃkhyais tad adhigamyate
ekaṃ sāṃkhyaṃ ca yogaṃ ca yaḥ paśyati sa tattvavit

43. anye ca yogino viprā aiśvaryāsaktacetasaḥ
majjanti tatra tatraiva na tv ātmaiṣām iti śrutiḥ[11]

44. yat tat sarvagataṃ divyam aiśvaryam acalaṃ mahat
jñānayogābhiyuktas tu dehānte tad avāpnuyāt

45. eṣa ātmāham avyakto māyāvī parameśvaraḥ
kīrtitaḥ sarvavedeṣu sarvātmā sarvatomukhaḥ

46. sarvakāmaḥ sarvarasaḥ sarvagandho 'jaro 'maraḥ
sarvataḥ pāṇipādo 'ham antaryāmī sanātanaḥ

47. apāṇipādo javano grahītā hṛdi saṃsthitaḥ
acakṣur api paśyāmi tathākarṇaḥ śṛṇomy aham

48. vedāhaṃ sarvam evedaṃ na māṃ jānāti kaścana
prāhur mahāntaṃ puruṣaṃ mām ekaṃ tattvadarśinaḥ

49. paśyanti ṛṣayo hetum ātmanaḥ sūkṣmadarśinaḥ
nirguṇāmalarūpasya yat tad aiśvaryam uttamam

50. yan na devā vijānanti mohitā mama māyayā
vakṣye samāhitā yūyaṃ śṛṇudhvaṃ brahmavādinaḥ

51. nāhaṃ praśāstā sarvasya māyātītaḥ svabhāvataḥ
prerayāmi tathāpīdaṃ kāraṇaṃ sūrayo viduḥ

52. yan me guhyatamaṃ dehaṃ sarvagaṃ tattvadarśinaḥ
praviṣṭā mama sāyujyaṃ labhante yogino 'vyayam

53. teṣāṃ hi vaśam āpannā māyā me viśvarūpiṇī
labhante paramāṃ śuddhiṃ nirvāṇaṃ te mayā saha

54. na teṣāṃ punarāvṛttiḥ kalpakoṭiśatair api
prasādān mama yogīndrā etad vedānuśāsanam

55. nāputraśiṣyayogibhyo dātavyaṃ brahmavādibhiḥ
maduktam etad vijñānaṃ sāṃkhyayogasamāśrayam

Chapter 3

Īśvara uvāca

1. avyaktād abhavat kālaḥ pradhānaṃ puruṣaḥ paraḥ
tebhyaḥ sarvam idaṃ jātaṃ tasmād brahmamayaṃ jagat

2. sarvataḥ pāṇipādaṃ tat sarvato 'kṣiśiromukham
sarvataḥ śrutimal loke sarvam āvṛtya tiṣṭhati

3. sarvendriyaguṇābhāsaṃ sarvendriyavivarjitam
sarvādhāraṃ sadānandam avyaktaṃ dvaitavarjitam

4. sarvopamānarahitaṃ pramāṇātītagocaram
nirvikalpaṃ nirābhāsaṃ sarvāvāsaṃ parāmṛtam

5. abhinnaṃ bhinnasaṃsthānaṃ śāśvataṃ dhruvam avyayam
nirguṇaṃ paramaṃ vyoma taj jñānaṃ sūrayo viduḥ

6. sa ātmā sarvabhūtānāṃ sa bāhyābhyantaraḥ paraḥ
so 'haṃ sarvatragaḥ śānto jñānātmā parameśvaraḥ

7. mayā tatam idaṃ viśvaṃ jagad avyaktamūrtinā
matsthāni sarvabhūtāni yas taṃ veda sa vedavit

8. pradhānaṃ puruṣaṃ caiva tattvadvayam udāhṛtam
tayor anādir uddiṣṭaḥ kālaḥ saṃyojakaḥ paraḥ

9. trayam etad anādyantam avyakte samavasthitam
tadātmakaṃ tadanyat syāt tad rūpaṃ māmakaṃ viduḥ

10. mahadādyaṃ viśeṣāntaṃ saṃprasūte 'khilaṃ jagat
yā sā prakṛtir uddiṣṭā mohinī sarvadehinām

11. puruṣaḥ prakṛtistho hi bhuṅkte yaḥ prākṛtān guṇān
ahaṃkāravimuktatvāt procyate pañcaviṃśakaḥ

12. ādyo vikāraḥ prakṛter mahān ātmeti kathyate
vijñānaśaktir vijñātā hy ahaṃkāras tadutthitaḥ

13. eka eva mahān ātmā so 'haṃkāro 'bhidhīyate
sa jīvaḥ so 'ntarātmeti gīyate tattvacintakaiḥ

14. tena vedayate sarvaṃ sukhaṃ duḥkhaṃ ca janmasu
sa vijñānātmakas tasya manaḥ syād upakārakam

15. tenāvivekatas tasmāt saṃsāraḥ puruṣasya tu
sa cāvivekaḥ prakṛtau saṅgāt kālena so 'bhavat

16. kālaḥ sṛjati bhūtāni kālaḥ saṃharati prajāḥ
sarve kālasya vaśagā na kālaḥ kasyacid vaśe

17. so 'ntarā sarvam evedaṃ niyacchati sanātanaḥ
procyate bhagavān prāṇaḥ sarvajñaḥ puruṣottamaḥ

18. sarvendriyebhyaḥ paramaṃ mana āhur manīṣiṇaḥ
manasaś cāpy ahaṃkāram ahaṃkārān mahān paraḥ

19. mahataḥ param avyaktam avyaktāt puruṣaḥ paraḥ
puruṣād bhagavān prāṇas tasya sarvam idaṃ jagat

20. prāṇāt parataraṃ vyoma vyomātīto 'gnir īśvaraḥ
so 'haṃ sarvatragaḥ śānto jñānātmā parameśvaraḥ
nāsti mattaḥ paraṃ bhūtaṃ māṃ vijñāya vimucyate

21. nityaṃ hi nāsti jagati bhūtaṃ sthāvarajaṅgamam
ṛte mām ekam avyaktaṃ vyomarūpaṃ maheśvaram

22. so 'haṃ sṛjāmi sakalaṃ saṃharāmi sadā jagat
māyī māyāmayaṃ devaḥ kālena saha saṅgataḥ[12]

23. matsannidhāv eṣa kālaḥ karoti sakalaṃ jagat
niyojayaty anantātmā hy etad vedānuśāsanam

Chapter 4

īśvara uvāca

1. vakṣye samāhitā yūyaṃ śṛṇudhvaṃ brahmavādinaḥ
māhātmyaṃ devadevasya yenedaṃ saṃpravartate[13]

2. nāhaṃ tapobhir vividhair na dānena na cejyayā
śakyo hi puruṣair jñātum ṛte bhaktim anuttamām

3. ahaṃ hi sarvabhāvānām antas tiṣṭhāmi sarvagaḥ
māṃ sarvasākṣiṇaṃ loko na jānāti munīśvarāḥ

4. yasyāntarā sarvam idaṃ yo hi sarvāntaraḥ paraḥ
so 'haṃ dhātā vidhātā ca kālāgnir viśvatomukhaḥ[14]

5. na māṃ paśyanti munayaḥ sarve 'pi tridivaukasaḥ
brahmā ca manavaḥ śakro ye cānye prathitaujasaḥ

6. gṛṇanti satataṃ vedā mām ekaṃ parameśvaram
yajanti vividhair agniṃ brāhmaṇā vaidikair makhaiḥ

7. sarve lokā namasyanti brahmā lokapitāmahaḥ
dhyāyanti yogino devaṃ bhūtādhipatim īśvaram

8. ahaṃ hi sarvahaviṣāṃ bhoktā caiva phalapradaḥ
sarvadevatanur bhūtvā sarvātmā sarvasaṃsthitaḥ

9. māṃ paśyantīha vidvāṃso dhārmikā vedavādinaḥ
teṣāṃ sannihito nityaṃ ye bhaktyā mām upāsate

10. brāhmaṇāḥ kṣatriyā vaiśyā dhārmikā mām upāsate
teṣāṃ dadāmi tat sthānam ānandaṃ paramaṃ padam

11. anye 'pi ye vikarmasthāḥ śūdrādyā nīcajātayaḥ
bhaktimantaḥ pramucyante kālena mayi saṃgatāḥ

12. na madbhaktā vinaśyanti madbhaktā vītakalmaṣāḥ
ādāv etat pratijñātaṃ na me bhaktaḥ praṇaśyati

13. yo vai nindati taṃ mūḍho devadevaṃ sa nindati
yo hi taṃ pūjayed bhaktyā sa pūjayati māṃ sadā

14. patraṃ puṣpaṃ phalaṃ toyaṃ madārādhanakāraṇāt
yo me dadāti niyataṃ sa me bhaktaḥ priyo mataḥ[15]

15. ahaṃ hi jagatām ādau brahmāṇaṃ parameṣṭhinam
vidhāya dattavān vedān aśeṣān ātmaniḥsṛtān

16. aham eva hi sarveṣāṃ yogināṃ gurur avyayaḥ
dhārmikāṇāṃ ca goptā 'haṃ nihantā vedavidviṣām

17. ahaṃ vai sarvasaṃsārān mocako yoginām iha
saṃsārahetur evāhaṃ sarvasaṃsāravarjitaḥ

18. aham eva hi saṃhartā sraṣṭāhaṃ paripālakaḥ
māyāvī māmikā śaktir māyā lokavimohinī

19. mamaiva ca parā śaktir yā sā vidyeti gīyate
nāśayāmi tayā māyāṃ yogināṃ hṛdi saṃsthitaḥ[16]

20. ahaṃ hi sarvaśaktīnāṃ pravartakanivartakaḥ
ādhārabhūtaḥ sarvāsāṃ nidhānam amṛtasya ca

21. ekā sarvāntarā śaktiḥ karoti vividhaṃ jagat
āsthāya brahmāṇo rūpaṃ manmayī madadhiṣṭhitā

22. anyā ca śaktir vipulā saṃsthāpayati me jagat
bhūtvā nārāyaṇo 'nanto jagannātho jaganmayaḥ

23. tṛtīyā mahatī śaktir nihanti sakalaṃ jagat
tāmasī me samākhyātā kālākhyā rudrarūpiṇī

24. dhyānena māṃ prapaśyanti kecij jñānena cāpare
apare bhaktiyogena karmayogena cāpare

25. sarveṣām eva bhaktānām iṣṭaḥ priyataro mama
yo hi jñānena māṃ nityam ārādhayati nānyathā

26. anye ca ye trayo bhaktā madārādhanakāṅkṣiṇaḥ
te 'pi māṃ prāpnuvanty eva nāvartante ca vai punaḥ

27. mayā tatam idaṃ kṛtsanaṃ pradhānapuruṣātmakam
mayy eva saṃsthitaṃ viśvaṃ mayā saṃpreryate jagat

28. nāhaṃ prerayitā viprāḥ paramaṃ yogam āśritaḥ
prerayāmi jagat kṛtsnam etad yo veda so 'mṛtaḥ

29. paśyāmy aśeṣam evedaṃ vartamānaṃ svabhāvataḥ
karoti kālo bhagavān mahāyogeśvaraḥ svayam

30. yogaḥ saṃprocyate yogī māyā śāstreṣu sūribhiḥ
yogeśvaro 'sau bhagavān mahādevo mahān prabhuḥ

31. mahattvaṃ sarvatattvānāṃ paratvāt parameṣṭhinaḥ
procyate bhagavān brahmā mahān brahmamayo 'malaḥ

32. yo mām evaṃ vijānāti mahāyogeśvareśvaram
so 'vikalpena yogena yujyate nātra saṃśayaḥ

33. so 'haṃ prerayitā devaḥ paramānandam āśritaḥ
nṛtyāmi yogī satataṃ yas tad veda sa vedavit

34. iti guhyatamaṃ jñānaṃ sarvavedeṣu niṣṭhitam
prasannacetase deyaṃ dhārmikāyāhitāgnaye

Chapter 5

vyāsa uvāca

1. etāvad uktvā bhagavān yogināṃ parameśvaraḥ
nanarta paramaṃ bhāvam aiśvaraṃ saṃpradarśayan

2. taṃ te dadṛśur īśānaṃ tejasāṃ paramaṃ nidhim
nṛtyamānaṃ mahādevaṃ viṣṇunā gagane 'male

3. yaṃ vidur yogatattvajñā yogino yatamānasāḥ
tam īśaṃ sarvabhūtānām ākaśe dadṛśuḥ kila

4. yasya māyāmayaṃ sarvaṃ yenedaṃ preryate jagat
nṛtyamānaḥ svayaṃ viprair viśveśaḥ khalu dṛśyate

5. yatpādapaṅkajaṃ smṛtvā puruṣo 'jñānajaṃ bhayam
jahati nṛtyamānaṃ taṃ bhūteśaṃ dadṛśuḥ kila[17]

6. yaṃ vinidrā jitaśvāsāḥ śāntā bhaktisamanvitāḥ
jyotirmayaṃ prapaśyanti sa yogī dṛśyate kila

7. yo 'jñānān mocayet kṣipraṃ prasanno bhaktavatsalaḥ
tam eva mocakaṃ rudram ākāśe dadṛśuḥ param

8. sahasraśirasaṃ devaṃ sahasracaraṇākṛtim
sahasrabāhuṃ jaṭilaṃ candrārdhakṛtaśekharam

9. vasānaṃ carma vaiyāghraṃ śūlāsaktamahākaram
daṇḍapāṇiṃ trayīnetraṃ sūryasomāgnilocanam

10. brahmāṇḍaṃ tejasā svena sarvam āvṛtya ca sthitam
daṃṣṭrākarālaṃ durdharṣaṃ sūryakoṭisamaprabham

11. aṇḍasthaṃ cāṇḍabāhyasthaṃ bāhyam abhyantaraṃ param
sṛjantam analajvālaṃ dahantam akhilaṃ jagat
nṛtyantaṃ dadṛśur devaṃ viśvakarmāṇam īśvaram

12. mahādevaṃ mahāyogaṃ devānām api daivatam
paśūnāṃ patim īśānaṃ jyotiṣāṃ jyotir avyayam

13. pinākinaṃ viśālākṣaṃ bheṣajaṃ bhavarogiṇām
kālātmānaṃ kālakālaṃ devadevaṃ maheśvaram

14. umāpatiṃ virūpākṣaṃ yogānandamayaṃ param
jñānavairāgyanilayaṃ jñānayogaṃ sanātanam

15. śāśvataiśvaryavibhavaṃ dharmādhāraṃ durāsadam
mahendropendranamitaṃ maharṣigaṇavanditam

16. ādhāraṃ sarvaśaktīnāṃ mahāyogeśvareśvaram
yogināṃ paramaṃ brahma yogināṃ yogavanditam
yogināṃ hṛdi tiṣṭhantaṃ yogamāyāsamāvṛtam

17. kṣaṇena jagato yoniṃ nārāyaṇam anāmayam
īśvareṇaikatāpannam apaśyan brahmavādinaḥ

18. dṛṣṭvā tad aiśvaraṃ rūpaṃ rudranārāyaṇātmakam
kṛtārthaṃ menire santaḥ svātmānaṃ brahmavādinaḥ

19. sanatkumāraḥ sanako bhṛguś ca
sanātanaś caiva sanandanaś ca
rudro 'ṅgirā vāmadevā tha śukro
maharṣir atriḥ kapilo marīciḥ

20. dṛṣṭvātha rudraṃ jagadīśitāraṃ
taṃ padmanābhāśritavāmabhāgam
dhyātvā hṛdisthaṃ praṇipatya mūrdhnā
baddhvāñjaliṃ sveṣu śiraḥsu bhūyaḥ

21. oṅkāram uccārya vilokya devam
antaḥśarīre nihitaṃ guhāyām
samastuvan brahmamayair vacobhir
ānandapūrṇāyatamānasās te munaya ūcuḥ

22. tvām ekam īśaṃ puruṣaṃ purāṇaṃ
prāṇeśvaraṃ rudram anantayogam
namāma sarve hṛdi sanniviṣṭaṃ
pracetasaṃ brahmamayaṃ pavitram

23. tvāṃ paśyanti munayo brahmayoniṃ
dāntāḥ śāntā vimalaṃ rukmavarṇam
dhyātvātmastham acalaṃ sve śarīre
kaviṃ parebhyaḥ paramaṃ paraṃ ca[18]

24. tvattaḥ prasūtā jagataḥ prasūtiḥ
sarvātmabhūs tvaṃ paramāṇubhūtaḥ
aṇor aṇīyān mahato mahīyāṃs
tvām eva sarvaṃ pravadanti santaḥ

25. hiraṇyagarbho jagadantarātmā
tvatto 'dhijātaḥ puruṣaḥ purāṇaḥ
saṃjāyamāno bhavatā visṛṣṭo
yathāvidhānaṃ sakalaṃ sasarja

26. tvatto vedāḥ sakalāḥ saṃprasūtās
tvayy evānte saṃsthitiṃ te labhante
paśyāmas tvāṃ jagato hetubhūtaṃ
nṛtyantaṃ sve hṛdaye sanniviṣṭam

27. tvayaivedaṃ bhrāmyate brahmacakraṃ
māyāvī tvaṃ jagatām ekanāthaḥ
namāmas tvāṃ śaraṇaṃ saṃprapannā
yogātmānaṃ citpatiṃ divyanṛtyam

28. paśyāmas tvāṃ paramākāśamadhye
nṛtyantaṃ te mahimānaṃ smarāmaḥ
sarvātmānaṃ bahudhā sanniviṣṭaṃ
brahmānandam anubhūyānubhūya

29. oṃkāras te vācako muktibījaṃ
tvam akṣaraṃ prakṛtau gūḍharūpam
tat tvāṃ satyaṃ pravadantīha santaḥ
svayaṃprabhaṃ bhavato yatprakāśam

30. stuvanti tvāṃ satataṃ sarvavedā
namanti tvām ṛṣayaḥ kṣīṇadoṣāḥ
śāntātmānaḥ satyasaṃdhā variṣṭhaṃ
viśanti tvāṃ yatayo brahmaniṣṭhāḥ

31. eko vedo bahuśākho hy anantas
tvām evaikaṃ bodhayaty ekarūpam
vedyaṃ tvāṃ śaraṇaṃ ye prapannās
teṣāṃ śāntiḥ śāśvatī netareṣām

32. bhavānīśo 'nādimāṃs tejorāśir
brahmā viṣṇuḥ parameṣṭhī variṣṭhaḥ
svātmānandam anubhūyādhiśete
svayaṃ jyotir acalo nityamuktaḥ[19]

33. eko rudras tvaṃ karoṣīha viśvaṃ
tvaṃ pālayasy akhilaṃ viśvarūpaḥ
tvām evānte nilayaṃ vindatīdaṃ
namāmas tvāṃ śaraṇaṃ saṃprapannāḥ

34. tvām ekam āhuḥ kavim ekarudraṃ
prāṇaṃ bṛhantaṃ harim agnim īśam

indraṃ mṛtyum anilaṃ cekitānaṃ
dhātāram ādityam anekarūpam

35. tvam akṣaraṃ paramaṃ veditavyaṃ
tvam asya viśvasya paraṃ nidhānam
tvam avyayaḥ śāśvatadharmagoptā
sanātanas tvaṃ puruṣottamo 'si

36. tvam eva viṣṇuś caturānanas tvaṃ
tvam eva rudro bhagavān adhīśaḥ
tvaṃ viśvanābhiḥ prakṛtiḥ pratiṣṭhā
sarveśvaras tvaṃ parameśvaro 'si

37. tvām ekam āhuḥ puruṣaṃ purāṇam
ādityavarṇaṃ tamasaḥ parastāt
cinmātram avyaktam acintyarūpaṃ
khaṃ brahma śūnyaṃ prakṛtiṃ nirguṇaṃ ca

38. yadantarā sarvam idaṃ vibhāti
yad avyayaṃ nirmalam ekarūpam
kim apy acintyaṃ tava rūpam etat
tadantarā yat pratibhāti tattvam

39. yogeśvaraṃ rudram anantaśaktiṃ
parāyaṇaṃ brahmatanuṃ pavitram
namāma sarve śaraṇārthinas tvāṃ
prasīda bhūtādhipate maheśa

40. tvatpādapadmasmaraṇād aśeṣa-
saṃsārabījaṃ vilayaṃ prayāti
mano niyamya praṇidhāya kāyaṃ
prasādayāmo vayam ekam īśam

41. namo bhavāyāstu bhavodbhavāya
kālāya sarvāya harāya tubhyaṃ
namo 'stu rudrāya kapardine te
namo 'gnaye deva namaḥ śivāya

42. tataḥ sa bhagavān devaḥ kapardī vṛṣavāhanaḥ
saṃhṛtya paramaṃ rūpaṃ prakṛtistho 'bhavad bhavaḥ

43. te bhavaṃ bhūtabhavyeśaṃ pūrvavat samavasthitam
dṛṣṭvā nārāyaṇaṃ devaṃ vismitā vākyam abruvan

44. bhagavan bhūtabhavyeśa govṛṣāṅkitaśāsana
dṛṣṭvā te paramaṃ rūpaṃ nirvṛtāḥ smaḥ sanātana[20]

45. bhavatprasādād amale parasmin parameśvare
asmākaṃ jāyate bhaktis tvayy evāvyabhicāriṇī

46. idānīṃ śrotum icchāmo māhātmyaṃ tava śaṅkara
bhūyo 'pi tava yan nityaṃ yāthātmyaṃ parameṣṭhinaḥ

47. sa teṣāṃ vākyam ākarṇya yogināṃ yogasiddhidaḥ
prāha gambhīrayā vācā samālokya ca mādhavam[21]

Chapter 6

īśvara uvāca

1. śṛṇudhvam ṛṣayaḥ sarve yathāvat parameṣṭhinaḥ
vakṣyāmīśasya māhātmyaṃ yat tad vedavido viduḥ

2. sarvalokaikanirmātā sarvalokaikarakṣitā
sarvalokaikasaṃhartā sarvātmāhaṃ sanātanaḥ

3. sarveṣām eva vastūnām antaryāmī pitā hy aham
madhye cāntaḥsthitaṃ sarvaṃ nāhaṃ sarvatra saṃsthitaḥ

4. bhavadbhir adbhutaṃ dṛṣṭaṃ yat svarūpaṃ tu māmakam
mamaiṣā hy upamā viprā māyayā darśitā mayā

5. sarveṣām eva bhāvānām antarā samavasthitaḥ
prerayāmi jagat kṛtsnaṃ kriyāśāktir iyaṃ mama

6. yayedaṃ ceṣṭate viśvaṃ tatsvabhāvānuvarti ca
so 'haṃ kālo jagat kṛtsnaṃ prerayāmi kalātmakam

7. ekāṃśena jagat kṛtsnaṃ karomi munipuṅgavāḥ
saṃharāmy ekarūpeṇa dvidhāvasthā mamaiva tu

8. ādimadhyāntanirmukto māyātattvapravartakaḥ
kṣobhayāmi ca sargādau pradhānapuruṣāv ubhau

9. tābhyāṃ saṃjāyate viśvaṃ saṃyuktābhyāṃ parasparam
mahadādikrameṇaiva mama tejo vijṛmbhate

10. yo hi sarvajagatsākṣī kālacakrapravartakaḥ
hiraṇyagarbho mārtaṇḍaḥ so 'pi maddehasaṃbhavaḥ

11. tasmai divyaṃ svam aiśvaryaṃ jñānayogaṃ sanātanam
dattavān ātmajān vedān kalpādau caturo dvijāḥ

12. sa manniyogato devo brahmā madbhāvabhāvitaḥ
divyaṃ tan māmakaiśvaryaṃ sarvadā vahati svayam

13. sa sarvalokanirmātā manniyogena sarvavit
bhūtvā caturmukhaḥ sargaṃ sṛjaty evātmasaṃbhavaḥ

14. yo 'pi nārāyaṇo 'nanto lokānāṃ prabhavo 'vyayaḥ
mamaiva paramā mūrtiḥ karoti paripālanam[22]

15. yo 'ntakaḥ sarvabhūtānāṃ rudraḥ kālātmakaḥ prabhuḥ
madājñayāsau satataṃ saṃhariṣyati me tanuḥ

16. havyaṃ vahati devānāṃ kavyaṃ kavyāśinām api
pākaṃ ca kurute vahniḥ so 'pi macchakticoditaḥ

17. bhuktam āhārajātaṃ ca pacate tad aharniśam
vaiśvānaro 'gnir bhagavān īśvarasya niyogataḥ

18. yo 'pi sarvāmbhasāṃ yonir varuṇo devapuṅgavaḥ
so 'pi saṃjīvayet kṛtsnam īśasyaiva niyogataḥ

19. yo 'ntas tiṣṭhati bhūtānāṃ bahir devaḥ prabhañjanaḥ
madājñayāsau bhūtānāṃ śarīrāṇi bibharti hi

20. yo 'pi saṃjīvano nṝṇāṃ devānām amṛtākaraḥ
somaḥ sa manniyogena coditaḥ kila vartate

21. yaḥ svabhāsā jagat kṛtsnaṃ prakāśayati sarvadā
sūryo vṛṣṭiṃ vitanute śāstreṇaiva svayaṃbhuvaḥ

22. yo 'py aśeṣajagacchāstā śakraḥ sarvāmareśvaraḥ
yajvanāṃ phalado devo vartate 'sau madājñayā

23. yaḥ praśāstā hy asādhūnāṃ vartate niyamād iha
yamo vaivasvato devo devadevaniyogataḥ

24. yo 'pi sarvadhanādhyakṣo dhanānāṃ saṃpradāyakaḥ
so 'pīśvaraniyogena kubero vartate sadā

25. yaḥ sarvarakṣasāṃ nāthas tāmasānāṃ phalapradaḥ
manniyogād asau devo vartate nirṛtiḥ sadā

26. vetālagaṇabhūtānāṃ svāmī bhogaphalapradaḥ
īśānaḥ kila bhaktānāṃ so 'pi tiṣṭhan mamājñayā

27. yo vāmadevo 'ṅgirasaḥ śiṣyo rudragaṇāgraṇīḥ
rakṣako yogināṃ nityaṃ vartate 'sau madājñayā

28. yaś ca sarvajagatpūjyo vartate vighnakārakaḥ
vināyako dharmanetā so 'pi madvacanāt kila

29. yo 'pi brahmavidāṃ śreṣṭho devasenāpatiḥ prabhuḥ
skando 'sau vartate nityaṃ svayambhūvidhicoditaḥ[23]

30. ye ca prajānāṃ patayo marīcyādyā maharṣayaḥ
sṛjanti vividhaṃ lokaṃ parasyaiva niyogataḥ

31. yā ca śrīḥ sarvabhūtānāṃ dadāti vipulāṃ śriyam
patnī nārāyaṇasyāsau vartate madanugrahāt

32. vācaṃ dadāti vipulāṃ yā ca devī sarasvatī
sāpīśvaraniyogena coditā saṃpravartate

33. yāśeṣapuruṣān ghorān narakāt tārayiṣyati
sāvitrī saṃsmṛtā devī devājñānuvidhāyinī

34. pārvatī paramā devī brahmavidyāpradāyinī
yāpi dhyātā viśeṣeṇa sāpi madvacanānugā

35. yo 'nantamahimānantaḥ śeṣo 'śeṣāmaraprabhuḥ
dadhāti śirasā lokaṃ so 'pi devaniyogataḥ

36. yo 'gniḥ saṃvartako nityaṃ vaḍavārūpasaṃsthitaḥ
pibaty akhilam ambhodhim īśvarasya niyogataḥ

37. ye caturdaśa loke 'smin manavaḥ prathitaujasaḥ
pālayanti prajāḥ sarvās te 'pi tasya niyogataḥ

38. ādityā vasavo rudrā marutaś ca tathāśvinau
anyāś ca devatāḥ sarvā macchāstreṇaiva dhiṣṭhitāḥ

39. gandharvā garuḍā ṛkṣāḥ siddhāḥ sādhyāś ca cāraṇāḥ
yakṣarakṣaḥ piśācāś ca sthitāḥ śāstre svayaṃbhuvaḥ

40. kalākāṣṭhānimeṣāś ca muhūrtā divasāḥ kṣapāḥ
ṛtavaḥ pakṣamāsāś ca sthitāḥ śāstre prajāpateḥ

41. yugamanvantarāṇy eva mama tiṣṭhanti śāsane
parāś caiva parārdhāś ca kālabhedās tathā pare

42. caturvidhāni bhūtāni sthāvarāṇi carāṇi ca
niyogād eva vartante devasya paramātmanaḥ

43. pātālāni ca sarvāṇi bhuvanāni ca śāsanāt
brahmāṇḍāni ca vartante sarvāṇy eva svayaṃbhuvaḥ

44. atītāny apy asaṃkhyāni brahmāṇḍāni mamājñayā
pravṛttāni padārthaughaiḥ sahitāni samantataḥ

45. brahmāṇḍāni bhaviṣyanti saha vastubhir ātmagaiḥ
vahiṣyanti sadaivājñāṃ parasya paramātmanaḥ

46. bhūmir āpo 'nalo vāyuḥ khaṃ mano buddhir eva ca
bhūtādir ādiprakṛtir niyoge mama vartate

47. yāśeṣajagatāṃ yonir mohinī sarvadehinām
māyā vivartate nityaṃ sāpīśvaraniyogataḥ

48. yo vai dehabhṛtāṃ devaḥ puruṣaḥ paṭhyate paraḥ
ātmāsau vartate nityam īśvarasya niyogataḥ

49. vidhūya mohakalilaṃ yayā paśyati tat padam
sāpi vidyā maheśasya niyogavaśavartinī

50. bahunātra kim uktena mama śaktyātmakaṃ jagat
mayaiva preryate kṛtsnaṃ mayy eva pralayaṃ vrajet

51. ahaṃ hi bhagavān īśaḥ svayaṃ jyotiḥ sanātanaḥ
paramātmā paraṃ brahma matto hy anyan na vidyate

52. ity etat paramaṃ jñānaṃ yuṣmākaṃ kathitaṃ mayā
jñātvā vimucyate jantur janmasaṃsārabandhanāt

Chapter 7

īśvara uvāca

1. śṛṇudhvam ṛṣayaḥ sarve prabhāvaṃ parameṣṭhinaḥ
yaṃ jñātvā puruṣo mukto na saṃsāre patet punaḥ

2. parāt parataraṃ brahma śāśvataṃ niṣkalaṃ dhruvam
nityānandaṃ nirvikalpaṃ tad dhāma paramaṃ mama

3. ahaṃ brahmavidāṃ brahmā svayaṃbhūr viśvatomukhaḥ
māyāvinām ahaṃ devaḥ purāṇo harir avyayaḥ

4. yoginām asmy ahaṃ śaṃbhuḥ strīṇāṃ devī girīndrajā
ādityānām ahaṃ viṣṇur vasūnām asmi pāvakaḥ

5. rudrāṇāṃ śaṃkaraś cāhaṃ garuḍaḥ patatām aham
airāvato gajendrāṇāṃ rāmaḥ śastrabhṛtām aham

6. ṛṣīṇāṃ ca vasiṣṭho 'haṃ devānāṃ ca śatakratuḥ
śilpināṃ viśvakarmāhaṃ prahlādo 'smy amaradviṣām

7. munīnām apy ahaṃ vyāso gaṇānāṃ ca vināyakaḥ
vīrāṇāṃ vīrabhadro 'haṃ siddhānāṃ kapilo muniḥ

8. parvatānām ahaṃ merur nakṣatrāṇāṃ ca candramāḥ
vajraṃ praharaṇānāṃ ca vratānāṃ satyam asmy aham

9. ananto bhogināṃ devaḥ senānīnāṃ ca pāvakiḥ
āśramāṇāṃ ca gārhastham īśvarāṇāṃ maheśvaraḥ

10. mahākalpaś ca kalpānāṃ yugānāṃ kṛtam asmy aham
kuberaḥ sarvayakṣāṇāṃ gaṇeśānāṃ ca vīrakaḥ

11. prajāpatīnāṃ dakṣo 'haṃ nirṛtiḥ sarvarakṣasām
vāyur balavatām asmi dvīpānāṃ puṣkaro 'smy aham

12. mṛgendrāṇāṃ ca siṃho 'haṃ yantrāṇāṃ dhanureva ca
vedānāṃ sāmavedo 'haṃ yajuṣāṃ śatarudriyam

13. sāvitrī sarvajapyānāṃ guhyānāṃ praṇavo 'smy aham
sūktānāṃ pauruṣaṃ sūktaṃ jyeṣṭhasāma ca sāmasu

14. sarvavedārthaviduṣāṃ manuḥ svāyaṃbhuvo 'smy aham
brahmāvartas tu deśānāṃ kṣetrāṇām avimuktakam

15. vidyānām ātmavidyāhaṃ jñānānām aiśvaraṃ param
bhūtānām asmy ahaṃ vyoma sattvānāṃ mṛtyur eva ca

16. pāśānām asmy ahaṃ māyā kālaḥ kalayatām aham
gatīnāṃ muktir evāhaṃ pareṣāṃ parameśvaraḥ

17. yac cānyad api loke 'smin sattvaṃ tejobalādhikam
tat sarvaṃ pratijānīdhvaṃ mama tejovijṛmbhitam

18. ātmānaḥ paśavaḥ proktāḥ sarve saṃsāravartinaḥ
teṣāṃ patir ahaṃ devaḥ smṛtaḥ paśupatir budhaiḥ

19. māyāpāśena badhnāmi paśūn etān svalīlayā
mām eva mocakaṃ prāhuḥ paśūnāṃ vedavādinaḥ

20. māyāpāśena baddhānāṃ mocako 'nyo na vidyate
mām ṛte paramātmānaṃ bhūtādhipatim avyayam

21. caturviṃśatitattvāni māyā karma guṇā iti
ete pāśāḥ paśupateḥ kleśāś ca paśubandhanāḥ

22. mano buddhir ahaṃkāraḥ khānilāgnijalāni bhūḥ
etāḥ prakṛtayas tv aṣṭau vikārāś ca tathāpare

23. śrotraṃ tvak cakṣuṣī jihvā ghrāṇaṃ caiva tu pañcamam
pāyūpasthaṃ karau pādau vāk caiva daśamī matā

24. śabdaḥ sparśaś ca rūpaṃ ca raso gandhas tathaiva ca
trayoviṃśatir etāni tattvāni prākṛtāni tu

25. caturviṃśakam avyaktaṃ pradhānaṃ guṇalakṣaṇam
anādimadhyanidhanaṃ kāraṇaṃ jagataḥ param

26. sattvaṃ rajas tamaś ceti guṇatrayam udāhṛtam
sāmyāvasthitim eteṣām avyaktaṃ prakṛtiṃ viduḥ

27. sattvaṃ jñānaṃ tamo 'jñānaṃ rajo miśram udāhṛtam
guṇānāṃ buddhivaiṣamyād vaiṣamyaṃ kavayo viduḥ

28. dharmādharmāv iti proktau pāśau dvau bandhasaṃjñitau
mayy arpitāni karmāṇi nibandhāya vimuktaye

29. avidyām asmitāṃ rāgaṃ dveṣaṃ cābhiniveśakam
kleśākhyān acalān prāhuḥ pāśān ātmanibandhanān

30. eteṣām eva pāśānāṃ māyā kāraṇam ucyate
mūlaprakṛtir avyaktā sā śaktir mayi tiṣṭhati

31. sa eva mūlaprakṛtiḥ pradhānaṃ puruṣo 'pi ca
vikārā mahadādīni devadevaḥ sanātanaḥ

32. sa eva bandhaḥ sa ca bandhakartā
sa eva pāśaḥ paśavaḥ sa eva
sa veda sarvaṃ na ca tasya vettā
tam āhur agryaṃ puruṣaṃ purāṇam

Chapter 8

īśvara uvāca

1. anyad guhyatamaṃ jñānaṃ vakṣye brāhmaṇapuṅgavāḥ
yenāsau tarate jantur ghoraṃ saṃsārasāgaram

2. ahaṃ brahmamayaḥ śāntaḥ śāśvato nirmalo 'vyayaḥ
ekākī bhagavān uktaḥ kevalaḥ parameśvaraḥ

3. mama yonir mahad brahma tatra garbhaṃ dadhāmy aham
mūlaṃ māyābhidhānaṃ tu tato jātam idaṃ jagat

4. pradhānaṃ puruṣo hy atmā mahān bhūtādir eva ca
tanmātrāṇi mahābhūtānīndriyāṇi ca jajñire

5. tato 'ṇḍam abhavad dhaimaṃ sūryakoṭisamaprabham
tasmin jajñe mahābrahmā macchaktyā copabṛṃhitaḥ

6. ye cānye bahavo jīvā manmayāḥ sarva eva te
na māṃ paśyanti pitaraṃ māyayā mama mohitāḥ

7. yāś ca yoniṣu sarvāsu saṃbhavanti hi mūrtayaḥ
tāsāṃ māyā parā yonir mām eva pitaraṃ viduḥ

8. yo mām evaṃ vijānāti bījinaṃ pitaraṃ prabhum
sa dhīraḥ sarvalokeṣu na moham adhigacchati

9. īśānaḥ sarvavidyānāṃ bhūtānāṃ parameśvaraḥ
oṅkāramūrtir bhagavān ahaṃ brahmā prajāpatiḥ

10. samaṃ sarveṣu bhūteṣu tiṣṭhantaṃ parameśvaram
vinaśyatsv avinaśyantaṃ yaḥ paśyati sa paśyati

11. samaṃ paśyan hi sarvatra samavasthitam īśvaram
na hinasty ātmanātmānaṃ tato yāti parāṃ gatim

12. viditvā sapta sūkṣmāṇi ṣaḍaṅgaṃ ca maheśvaram
pradhānaviniyogajñaḥ paraṃ brahmādhigacchati

13. sarvajñatā tṛptir anādibodhaḥ
svatantratā nityam aluptaśaktiḥ

anantaśaktiś ca vibhor viditvā
ṣaḍ āhur aṅgāni maheśvarasya

14. tanmātrāṇi mana ātmā ca tāni
sūkṣmāṇy āhuḥ sapta tattvātmakāni
yā sā hetuḥ prakṛtiḥ sā pradhānaṃ
bandhaḥ prokto viniyogo 'pi tena

15. yā sā śaktiḥ prakṛtau līnarūpā
vedeṣūktā kāraṇaṃ brahmayoniḥ
tasyā ekaḥ parameṣṭhī parastān
maheśvaraḥ puruṣaḥ satyarūpaḥ

16. brahmā yogī paramātmā mahīyān
vyomavyāpī vedavedyaḥ purāṇaḥ
eko rudro mṛtyur avyaktam ekaṃ
bījaṃ viśvaṃ deva ekaḥ sa eva

17. tam evaikaṃ prāhur anye 'py anekaṃ
tv ekātmānaṃ kecid anyat tathāhuḥ
aṇor aṇīyān mahato 'sau mahīyān
mahādevaḥ procyate vedavidbhiḥ

18. evaṃ hi yo veda guhāśayaṃ paraṃ
prabhuṃ purāṇaṃ puruṣaṃ viśvarūpam
hiraṇmayaṃ buddhimatāṃ parāṃ gatiṃ
sa buddhimān buddhim atītya tiṣṭhati

Chapter 9

ṛṣaya ūcuḥ

1. niṣkalo nirmalo nityo niṣkriyaḥ parameśvaraḥ
tan no vada mahādeva viśvarūpaḥ kathaṃ bhavān

īśvara uvāca

2. nāhaṃ viśvo na viśvaṃ ca māmṛte vidyate dvijāḥ
māyā nimittam atrāsti sā cātmānam upāśritā[24]

3. anādinidhanā śaktir māyāvyaktasamāśrayā
tannimittaḥ prapañco 'yam avyaktād abhavat khalu

4. avyaktaṃ kāraṇaṃ prāhur ānandaṃ jyotir akṣaram
aham eva paraṃ brahma matto hy anyan na vidyate

5. tasmān me viśvarūpatvaṃ niścitaṃ brahmavādibhiḥ
ekatve ca pṛthaktve ca proktam etan nidarśanam

6. ahaṃ tat paramaṃ brahma paramātmā sanātanaḥ
akāraṇaṃ dvijāḥ prokto na doṣo hy ātmanas tathā

7. anantāḥ śaktayo 'vyakte māyādyāḥ saṃsthitā dhruvāḥ
tasmin divi sthitaṃ nityam avyaktaṃ bhāti kevalam[25]

8. yābhis tal lakṣyate bhinnam abhinnaṃ tu svabhāvataḥ
ekayā mama sāyujyam anādinidhanaṃ dhruvam

9. puṃso 'bhūd anyayā bhūtir anyayā tattirohitam
anādimadhyanidhanaṃ yujyate 'vidyayā kila[26]

10. tad etat param avyaktaṃ prabhāmaṇḍalamaṇḍitam
tad akṣaraṃ paraṃ jyotis tad viṣṇoḥ paramaṃ padam[27]

11. tatra sarvam idaṃ protam otaṃ caivākhilaṃ jagat
tad eva ca jagat kṛtsnaṃ tad vijñāya vimucyate

12. yato vāco nivartante aprāpya manasā saha
ānandaṃ brahmaṇo vidvān bibheti na kutaścana[28]

13. vedāham etaṃ puruṣaṃ mahāntam
ādityavarṇaṃ tamasaḥ parastāt
tad vijñāya parimucyeta vidvān
nityānandī bhavati brahmabhūtaḥ

14. yasmāt paraṃ nāparam asti kiñcit
yaj jyotiṣāṃ jyotir ekaṃ divistham
tad evātmānaṃ manyamāno 'tha vidvān
ātmānandī bhavati brahmabhūtaḥ

15. tad avyayaṃ kalilaṃ gūḍhadehaṃ
brahmānandam amṛtaṃ viśvadhāma
vadanty evaṃ brāhmaṇā brahmaniṣṭhā
yatra gatvā na nivarteta bhūyaḥ

16. hiraṇmaye paramākāśatattve
yad arciṣi pravibhātīva tejaḥ
tad vijñāne paripaśyanti dhīrā
vibhrājamānaṃ vimalaṃ vyoma dhāma

17. tataḥ paraṃ paripaśyanti dhīrā
ātmany ātmānam anubhūyānubhūya
svayaṃprabhaḥ parameṣṭhī mahīyān
brahmānandī bhagavān īśa eṣaḥ

18. eko devaḥ sarvabhūteṣu gūḍhaḥ
sarvavyāpī sarvabhūtāntarātmā

tam evaikaṃ ye 'nupaśyanti dhīrās
teṣāṃ śāntiḥ śāśvatī netareṣām

19. sarvānanaśirogrīvaḥ sarvabhūtaguhāśayaḥ
sarvavyāpī ca bhagavān na tasmād anyad iṣyate

20. ity etad aiśvaraṃ jñānam uktaṃ vo munipuṅgavāḥ
gopanīyaṃ viśeṣeṇa yoginām api durlabham

Chapter 10

īśvara uvāca

1. aliṅgam ekam avyaktaṃ liṅgaṃ brahmeti niścitam
svayaṃjyotiḥ paraṃ tattvaṃ pare vyomni vyavasthitam

2. avyaktaṃ kāraṇaṃ yat tad akṣaraṃ paramaṃ padam
nirguṇaṃ śuddhavijñānaṃ tad vai paśyanti sūrayaḥ

3. tanniṣṭhāḥ śāntasaṃkalpā nityaṃ tadbhāvabhāvitāḥ
paśyanti tat paraṃ brahma yat tal liṅgam iti śrutiḥ

4. anyathā na hi māṃ draṣṭuṃ śakyaṃ vai munipuṅgavāḥ
na hi tad vidyate jñānaṃ yatas taj jñāyate param

5. etat tat paramaṃ jñānaṃ kevalaṃ kavayo viduḥ
ajñānam itarat sarvaṃ yasmān māyāmayaṃ jagat

6. yaj jñānaṃ nirmalaṃ sūkṣmaṃ nirvikalpaṃ yad avyayam
mamātmāsau tad evedam iti prāhur vipaścitaḥ

7. ye 'py anekaṃ prapaśyanti te 'pi paśyanti tat param
āśritāḥ paramāṃ niṣṭhāṃ buddhvaikaṃ tattvam avyayam

8. ye punaḥ paramaṃ tattvam ekaṃ vānekamīśvaram
bhaktyā māṃ saṃprapaśyanti vijñeyās te tadātmakāḥ

9. sākṣād eva prapaśyanti svātmānaṃ parameśvaram
nityānandaṃ nirvikalpaṃ satyarūpam iti sthitiḥ

10. bhajante paramānandaṃ sarvagaṃ yat tadātmakam
svātmany avasthitāḥ śāntāḥ pare 'vyakte parasya tu

11. eṣā vimuktiḥ paramā mama sāyujyam uttamam
nirvāṇaṃ brahmaṇā caikyaṃ kaivalyaṃ kavayo viduḥ

12. tasmād anādimadhyāntaṃ vastv ekaṃ paramaṃ śivam
sa īśvaro mahādevas taṃ vijñāya vimucyate

13. na tatra sūryaḥ pravibhātīha candro
na nakṣatrāṇi tapano nota vidyut
tadbhāsedam akhilaṃ bhāti nityaṃ
tannityabhāsam acalaṃ sad vibhāti

14. nityoditaṃ saṃvidā nirvikalpaṃ
śuddhaṃ bṛhantaṃ paramaṃ yad vibhāti
atrāntaraṃ brahmavido 'tha nityaṃ
paśyanti tattvam acalaṃ yat sa īśaḥ

15. nityānandam amṛtaṃ satyarūpaṃ
śuddhaṃ vadanti puruṣaṃ sarvavedāḥ
tam om iti praṇaveneśitāraṃ
dhāyāyanti vedārthaviniścitārthāḥ

16. na bhūmir āpo na mano na vahniḥ
prāṇo 'nilo gaganaṃ nota buddhiḥ
na cetano 'nyat paramākāśamadhye
vibhāti devaḥ śiva eva kevalaḥ

17. ity etad uktaṃ paramaṃ rahasyaṃ
jñānāmṛtaṃ sarvavedeṣu gūḍham
jānāti yogī vijane 'tha deśe
yuñjīta yogaṃ prayato hy ajasram

Chapter 11

īśvara uvāca

1. ataḥ paraṃ pravakṣyāmi yogaṃ paramadurlabham
yenātmānaṃ prapaśyanti bhānumantam iveśvaram

2. yogāgnir dahati kṣipram aśeṣaṃ pāpapañjaram
prasannaṃ jāyate jñānaṃ sākṣān nirvāṇasiddhidam

3. yogāt saṃjāyate jñānaṃ jñānād yogaḥ pravartate
yogajñānābhiyuktasya prasīdati maheśvaraḥ

4. ekakālaṃ dvikālaṃ vā trikālaṃ nityam eva vā
ye yuñjantīha madyogaṃ te vijñeyā maheśvarāḥ[29]

5. yogas tu dvividho jñeyo hy abhāvaḥ prathamo mataḥ
aparas tu mahāyogaḥ sarvayogottamottamaḥ

6. śūnyaṃ sarvanirābhāsaṃ svarūpaṃ yatra cintyate
abhāvayogaḥ sa prokto yenātmānaṃ prapaśyati

7. yatra paśyati cātmānaṃ nityānandaṃ nirañjanam
mayaikyaṃ sa mahāyogo bhāṣitaḥ parameśvaraḥ[30]

8. ye cānye yogināṃ yogāḥ śrūyante granthavistare
sarve te brahmayogasya kalāṃ nārhanti ṣoḍaśīm

9. yatra sākṣāt prapaśyanti vimuktā viśvam īśvaram
sarveṣām eva yogānāṃ sa yogaḥ paramo mataḥ

10. sahasraśo 'tha śataśo ye ceśvarabahiṣkṛtāḥ
na te paśyanti mām ekaṃ yogino yatamānasāḥ

11. prāṇāyāmas tathā dhyānaṃ pratyāhāro 'tha dhāraṇā
samādhiś ca muniśreṣṭhā yamo niyama āsanam

12. mayy ekacittatā yogo vṛttyantaranirodhataḥ
tatsādhanāny aṣṭadhā tu yuṣmākaṃ kathitāni tu[31]

13. ahiṃsā satyam asteyaṃ brahmacaryāparigrahau
yamāḥ saṃkṣepataḥ proktāś cittaśuddhipradā nṛṇām

14. karmaṇā manasā vācā sarvabhūteṣu sarvadā
akleśajananaṃ proktaṃ tv ahiṃsā paramarṣibhiḥ

15. ahiṃsāyāḥ paro dharmo nāsty ahiṃsā paraṃ sukham
vidhinā yā bhaved dhiṃsā tv ahiṃsaiva prakīrtitā

16. satyena sarvam āpnoti satye sarvaṃ pratiṣṭhitam
yathārthakathanācāraḥ satyaṃ proktaṃ dvijātibhiḥ

17. paradravyāpaharaṇaṃ cauryād vā 'tha balena vā
steyaṃ tasyānācaraṇād asteyaṃ dharmasādhanam

18. karmaṇā manasā vācā sarvāvasthāsu sarvadā
sarvatra maithunatyāgaṃ brahmacaryaṃ pracakṣate

19. dravyāṇām apy anādānam āpady api yathecchayā
aparigraha ity āhus taṃ prayatnena pālayet

20. tapaḥsvādhyāyasaṃtoṣāḥ śaucam īśvarapūjanam
samāsān niyamāḥ proktā yogasiddhipradāyinaḥ

21. upavāsaparākādikṛcchracāndrāyaṇādibhiḥ
śarīraśoṣaṇaṃ prāhus tāpasās tapa uttamam

22. vedāntaśatarudrīyapraṇavādijapaṃ budhāḥ
sattvaśuddhikaraṃ puṃsāṃ svādhyāyaṃ paricakṣate

23. svādhyāyasya trayo bhedā vācikopāṃśumānasāḥ
uttarottaravaiśiṣṭyaṃ prāhur vedārthavedinaḥ

24. yaḥ śabdabodhajananaḥ pareṣāṃ śṛṇvatāṃ sphuṭam
svādhyāyo vācikaḥ prokta upāṃśor atha lakṣaṇam

25. oṣṭhayoḥ spandamātreṇa parasyāśabdabodhakaḥ
upāṃśur eṣa nirdiṣṭaḥ sāhasro vācikāj japaḥ

26. yat padākṣarasaṅgatyā parispandanavarjitam
cintanaṃ sarvaśabdānāṃ mānasaṃ taṃ japaṃ viduḥ

27. yadṛcchālābhato nityam alaṃ puṃso bhaved iti
yā dhīs tām ṛṣayaḥ prāhuḥ saṃtoṣaṃ sukhalakṣaṇam

28. bāhyam ābhyantaraṃ śaucaṃ dvidhā proktaṃ dvijottamāḥ
mṛjjalābhyāṃ smṛtaṃ bāhyaṃ manaḥśuddhir athāntaram[32]

29. stutismaraṇapūjābhir vāṅmanaḥkāyakarmabhiḥ
suniścalā śive bhaktir etad īśvarapūjanam

30. yamāḥ saniyamāḥ proktāḥ prāṇāyāmaṃ nibodhata
prāṇaḥ svadehajo vāyur āyāmas tannirodhanam

31. uttamādhamamadhyatvāt tridhā 'yaṃ pratipāditaḥ
sa eva dvividhaḥ proktaḥ sagarbho 'garbha eva ca

32. mātrādvādaśako mandaś caturviṃśatimātrikaḥ
madhyamaḥ prāṇasaṃrodhaḥ ṣaṭtriṃśānmātrikottamaḥ

33. prasvedakampanotthānajanakatvaṃ yathākramam
mandamadhyamamukhyānām ānandād uttamottamaḥ

34. sagarbham āhuḥ sajapam agarbhaṃ vijapaṃ budhāḥ
etad vai yoginām uktaṃ prāṇāyāmasya lakṣaṇam

35. savyāhṛtiṃ sapraṇavāṃ gāyatrīṃ śirasā saha
trir japed āyataprāṇaḥ prāṇāyāmaḥ sa ucyate

36. recakaḥ pūrakaś caiva prāṇāyāmo 'tha kumbhakaḥ
procyate sarvaśāstreṣu yogibhir yatamānasaiḥ

37. recako 'jastraniśvāsāt pūrakas tannirodhataḥ
sāmyena saṃsthitir yā sā kumbhakaḥ parigīyate

38. indriyāṇāṃ vicaratāṃ viṣayeṣu svabhāvataḥ
nigrahaḥ procyate sadbhiḥ pratyāhāras tu sattamāḥ

39. hṛtpuṇḍarīke nābhyāṃ vā mūrdhni parvatamastake
evamādiṣu deśeṣu dhāraṇā cittabandhanam

40. deśāvasthitim ālambya buddher yā vṛttisaṃtatiḥ
vṛttyantarair asaṃsṛṣṭā tad dhyānaṃ sūrayo viduḥ

41. ekākāraḥ samādhiḥ syād deśālambanavarjitaḥ
pratyayo hy arthamātreṇa yogasādhanam uttamam

42. dhāraṇā dvādaśāyāmā dhyānaṃ dvādaśadhāraṇāḥ
dhyānaṃ dvādaśakaṃ yāvat samādhir abhidhīyate

43. āsanaṃ svastikaṃ proktaṃ padmam ardhāsanaṃ tathā
sādhanānāṃ ca sarveṣām etatsādhanam uttamam

44. ūrvor upari viprendrāḥ kṛtvā pādatale ubhe
samāsītātmanaḥ padmam etad āsanam uttamam

45. ekaṃ pādam athaikasmin vinyasyoruṇi sattamāḥ
āsītārdhāsanam idaṃ yogasādhanam uttamam

46. ubhe kṛtvā pādatale jānūrvor antareṇa hi
samāsītātmanaḥ proktam āsanaṃ svastikaṃ param

47. adeśakāle yogasya darśanaṃ hi na vidyate
agnyabhyāse jale vā 'pi śuṣkaparṇacaye tathā

48. jantuvyāpte śmaśāne ca jīrṇagoṣṭhe catuṣpathe
saśabde sabhaye vā 'pi caityavalmīkasaṃcaye

49. aśubhe durjanākrānte maśakādisamanvite
nācared dehabādhe vā daurmanasyādisaṃbhave

50. sugupte suśubhe deśe guhāyāṃ parvatasya tu
nadyāstīre puṇyadeśe devatāyatane tathā

51. gṛhe vā suśubhe ramye vijane jantuvarjite
yuñjīta yogī satatam ātmānaṃ matparāyaṇaḥ

52. namaskṛtya tu yogīndrān saśiṣyāṃś ca vināyakam
guruṃ caivātha māṃ yogī yuñjīta susamāhitaḥ

53. āsanaṃ svastikaṃ baddhvā padmam ardham athāpi vā
nāsikāgre samāṃ dṛṣṭim īṣadunmīliteksaṇaḥ

54. kṛtvātha nirbhayaḥ śāntas tyaktvā māyāmayaṃ jagat
svātmany avasthitaṃ devaṃ cintayet parameśvaram

55. śikhāgre dvādaśāṅgulye kalpayitvātha paṅkajam
dharmakandasamudbhūtaṃ jñānanālaṃ suśobhanam

56. aiśvaryāṣṭadalaṃ śvetaṃ paraṃ vairāgyakarṇikam
cintayet paramaṃ kośaṃ karṇikāyāṃ hiraṇmayam

57. sarvaśaktimayaṃ sākṣād yaṃ prāhur divyam avyayam
oṃkāravācyam avyaktaṃ raśmijālasamākulam

58. cintayet tatra vimalaṃ paraṃ jyotir yad akṣaram
tasmin jyotiṣi vinyasya svātmānaṃ tadabhedataḥ

59. dhyāyītākāśamadhyastham īśaṃ paramakāraṇam
tadātmā sarvago bhūtvā na kiñcid api cintayet

60. etad guhyatamaṃ dhyānaṃ dhyānāntaram athocyate
cintayitvā tu pūrvoktaṃ hṛdaye padmam uttamam

61. ātmānam atha kartāraṃ tatrānalasamatviṣam
madhye vahniśikhākāraṃ puruṣaṃ pañcaviṃśakam

62. cintayet paramātmānaṃ tanmadhye gaganaṃ param
oṃkārabodhitaṃ tattvaṃ śāśvataṃ śivam acyutam

63. avyaktaṃ prakṛtau līnaṃ paraṃ jyotir anuttamam
tadantaḥ paramaṃ tattvam ātmādhāraṃ nirañjanam

64. dhyāyīta tanmayo nityam ekarūpaṃ maheśvaram
viśodhya sarvatattvāni praṇavenāthavā punaḥ

65. saṃsthāpya mayi cātmānaṃ nirmale parame pade
plāvayitvātmano dehaṃ tenaiva jñānavāriṇā

66. madātmā manmayo bhasma gṛhītvā hy agnihotrajam
tenoddhṛtya tu sarvāṅgam agnir ityādimantrataḥ
cintayet svātmanīśānaṃ paraṃ jyotiḥsvarūpiṇam[33]

67. eṣa pāśupato yogaḥ paśupāśavimuktaye
sarvavedāntasāro 'yam atyāśramam iti śrutiḥ

68. etat paratarаṃ guhyaṃ matsāyujyopapādakam
dvijātīnāṃ tu kathitaṃ bhaktānāṃ brahmacāriṇām

69. brahmacaryam ahiṃsā ca kṣamā śaucaṃ tapo damaḥ
saṃtoṣaḥ satyam āstikyaṃ vratāṅgāni viśeṣataḥ

70. ekenāpy atha hīnena vratam asya tu lupyate
tasmād ātmaguṇopeto madvrataṃ voḍhum arhati

71. vītarāgabhayakrodhā manmayā mām upāśritāḥ
bahavo 'nena yogena pūtā madbhāvam āgatāḥ

72. ye yathā māṃ prapadyante tāṃs tathaiva bhajāmy aham
jñānayogena māṃ tasmād yajeta parameśvaram

73. athavā bhaktiyogena vairāgyeṇa pareṇa tu
cetasā bodhayuktena pūjayen māṃ sadā śuciḥ

74. sarvakarmāṇi saṃnyasya bhikṣāśī niṣparigrahaḥ
prāpnoti mama sāyujyaṃ guhyam etan mayoditam

75. adveṣṭā sarvabhūtānāṃ maitraḥ karuṇa eva ca
nirmamo nirahaṃkāro yo madbhaktaḥ sa me priyaḥ

76. saṃtuṣṭaḥ satataṃ yogī yatātmā dṛḍhaniścayaḥ
mayy arpitamanobuddhir yo madbhaktaḥ sa me priyaḥ[34]

77. yasmān nodvijate loko lokān nodvijate ca yaḥ
harṣāmarṣabhayodvegair mukto yaḥ sa hi me priyaḥ

78. anapekṣaḥ śucir dakṣa udāsīno gatavyathaḥ
sarvārambhaparityāgī bhaktimān yaḥ sa me priyaḥ

79. tulyanindāstutir maunī saṃtuṣṭo yena kenacit
aniketaḥ sthiramatir madbhakto mām upaiṣyati

80. sarvakarmāṇy api sadā kurvāṇo matparāyaṇaḥ
matprasādād avāpnoti śāśvataṃ paramaṃ padam

81. cetasā sarvakarmāṇi mayi saṃnyasya matparaḥ
nirāśīr nirmamo bhūtvā mām ekaṃ śaraṇaṃ vrajet

82. tyaktvā karmaphalāsaṅgaṃ nityatṛpto nirāśrayaḥ
karmaṇy abhipravṛtto 'pi naiva tena nibadhyate

83. nirāśīr yatacittātmā tyaktasarvaparigrahaḥ
śārīraṃ kevalaṃ karma kurvan nāpnoti tat padam

84. yadṛcchālābhatuṣṭasya dvandvātītasya caiva hi
kurvato matprasādārthaṃ karma saṃsāranāśanam

85. manmanā mannamaskāro madyājī matparāyaṇaḥ
mām upaiṣyati yogīśo jñātvā māṃ parameśvaram[35]

86. madbuddhayo māṃ satataṃ bodhayantaḥ parasparam
kathayantaś ca māṃ nityaṃ mama sāyujyam āpnuyuḥ

87. evaṃ nityābhiyuktānāṃ māyeyaṃ karmasānvagam
nāśayāmi tamaḥ kṛtsnaṃ jñānadīpena bhāsvatā

88. madbuddhayo māṃ satataṃ pūjayantīha ye janāḥ
teṣāṃ nityābhiyuktānāṃ yogakṣemaṃ vahāmy aham

89. ye 'nye ca kāmabhogārthaṃ yajante hy anyadevatāḥ
teṣāṃ tadantaṃ vijñeyaṃ devatānugataṃ phalam

90. ye cānyadevatābhaktāḥ pūjayantīha devatāḥ
madbhāvanāsamāyuktā mucyante te 'pi bhāvataḥ

91. tasmād anīśvarān anyāṃs tyaktvā devān aśeṣataḥ
mām eva saṃśrayed īśaṃ sa yāti paramaṃ padam

92. tyaktvā putrādiṣu snehaṃ niḥśoko niṣparigrahaḥ
yajec cāmaraṇāl liṅge viraktaḥ parameśvaram

93. ye 'rcayanti sadā liṅgaṃ tyaktvā bhogān aśeṣataḥ
ekena janmanā teṣāṃ dadāmi paramaiśvaram

94. parānandātmakaṃ liṅgaṃ kevalaṃ san nirañjanam
jñānātmakaṃ sarvagataṃ yogināṃ hṛdi saṃsthitam

95. ye cānye niyatā bhaktā bhāvayitvā vidhānataḥ
yatra kvacana tal liṅgam arcayanti maheśvaram

96. jale vā vahnimadhye vā vyomni sūrye 'thavā 'nyataḥ
ratnādau bhāvayitveśam arcayel liṅgam aiśvaram

97. sarvaṃ liṅgam ayaṃ hy etat sarvaṃ liṅge pratiṣṭhitam
tasmāl liṅge 'rcayed īśaṃ yatra kvacana śāśvatam

98. agnau kriyāvatām apsu vyomni sūrye manīṣiṇām
kāṣṭhādiṣv eva mūrkhāṇāṃ hṛdi liṅgaṃ tu yoginām

99. yady anutpannivijñāno viraktaḥ prītisaṃyutaḥ
yāvaj jīvaṃ japed yuktaḥ praṇavaṃ brahmaṇo vapuḥ

100. athavā śatarudrīyaṃ japed āmaraṇād dvijaḥ
ekākī yatacittātmā sa yāti paramaṃ padam

101. vased vāmaraṇād vipro vārāṇasyāṃ samāhitaḥ
so 'pīśvaraprasādena yāti tat paramaṃ padam

102. tatrotkramaṇakāle hi sarveṣām eva dehinām
dadāmi tat paraṃ jñānaṃ yena mucyeta bandhanāt[36]

103. varṇāśramavidhiṃ kṛtsnaṃ kurvāṇo matparāyaṇaḥ
tenaiva janmanā jñānaṃ labdhvā yāti śivaṃ padam

104. ye 'pi tatra vasantīha nīcā vā pāpayonayaḥ
sarve taranti saṃsāram īśvarānugrahād dvijāḥ

105. kintu vighnā bhaviṣyanti pāpopahatacetasām
dharmaṃ samāśrayet tasmān muktaye niyataṃ dvijāḥ

106. etad rahasyaṃ vedānāṃ na deyaṃ yasya kasyacit
dhārmikāyaiva dātavyaṃ bhaktāya brahmacāriṇe

vyāsa uvāca

107. ity etad uktvā bhagavān ātmayogam anuttamam
vyājahāra samāsīnaṃ nārāyaṇam anāmayam

108. mayaitad bhāṣitaṃ jñānaṃ hitārthaṃ brahmavādinām
dātavyaṃ śāntacittebhyaḥ śiṣyebhyo bhavatā śivam

109. uktvaivam atha yogīndrān abravīd bhagavān ajaḥ
hitāya sarvabhaktānāṃ dvijātīnāṃ dvijottamāḥ

110. bhavanto 'pi hi majjñānaṃ śiṣyāṇāṃ vidhipūrvakam
upadekṣyanti bhaktānāṃ sarveṣāṃ vacanān mama

111. ayaṃ nārāyaṇo yo 'haṃ īśvaro nātra saṃśayaḥ
nāntaraṃ ye prapaśyanti teṣāṃ deyam idaṃ param

112. mamaiṣā paramā mūrtir nārāyaṇasamāhvayā
sarvabhūtātmabhūtasthā śāntā cākṣarasaṃjñitā

113. ye tv anyathā prapaśyanti loke bhedadṛśo janāḥ
na te māṃ saṃprapaśyanti jāyante ca punaḥ punaḥ

114. ye tv imaṃ viṣṇum avyaktaṃ māṃ vā devaṃ maheśvaram
ekībhāvena paśyanti na teṣāṃ punarudbhavaḥ

115. tasmād anādinidhanaṃ viṣṇum ātmānam avyayam
mām eva saṃprapaśyadhvaṃ pūjayadhvaṃ tathaiva hi

116. ye 'nyathā māṃ prapaśyanti matvemaṃ devatāntaram
te yānti narakān ghorān nāhaṃ teṣu vyavasthitaḥ

117. mūrkhaṃ vā paṇḍitaṃ vāpi brāhmaṇaṃ vā madāśrayam
mocayāmi śvapākaṃ vā na nārāyaṇanindakam

118. tasmād eṣa mahāyogī madbhaktaiḥ puruṣottamaḥ
arcanīyo namaskāryo matprītijananāya hi

119. evam uktvā samāliṅgya vāsudevaṃ pinākadhṛk
antarhito 'bhavat teṣāṃ sarveṣām eva paśyatām

120. nārāyaṇo 'pi bhagavāṃs tāpasaṃ veṣam uttamam
jagrāha yoginaḥ sarvāṃs tyaktvā vai paramaṃ vapuḥ

121. jñātaṃ bhavadbhir amalaṃ prasādāt parameṣṭhinaḥ
sākṣād eva maheśasya jñānaṃ saṃsāranāśanam

122. gacchadhvaṃ vijvarāḥ sarve vijñānaṃ parameṣṭhinaḥ
pravartayadhvaṃ śiṣyebhyo dhārmikebhyo munīśvarāḥ

123. idaṃ bhaktāya śāntāya dhārmikāyāhitāgnaye
vijñānam aiśvaraṃ deyaṃ brāhmaṇāya viśeṣataḥ

124. evam uktvā sa viśvātmā yogināṃ yogavittamaḥ
nārāyaṇo mahāyogī jagāmādarśanaṃ svayam

125. te 'pi devādideveśaṃ namaskṛtya maheśvaram
nārāyaṇaṃ ca bhūtādiṃ svāni sthānāni bhejire

126. sanatkumāro bhagavān saṃvartāya mahāmuniḥ
dattavān aiśvaraṃ jñānaṃ so 'pi satyavratāya tu

127. sanandano 'pi yogīndraḥ pulahāya maharṣaye
pradadau gautamāyātha pulaho 'pi prajāpatiḥ

128. aṅgirā vedaviduṣe bharadvājāya dattavān
jaigīṣavyāya kapilas tathā pañcaśikhāya ca

129. parāśaro 'pi sanakāt pitā me sarvatattvadṛk
lebhe tat paramaṃ jñānaṃ tasmād vālmīkir āptavān

130. mamovāca purā devaḥ satīdehabhavāṅgajaḥ
vāmadevo mahāyogī rudraḥ kila pinākadhṛk

131. nārāyaṇo 'pi bhagavān devakītanayo hariḥ
arjunāya svayaṃ sākṣāt dattavān idam uttamam

132. yad ahaṃ labdhavān rudrād vāmadevād anuttamam
viśeṣād giriśe bhaktis tasmād ārabhya me 'bhavat[37]

133. śaraṇyaṃ śaraṇaṃ rudraṃ prapanno 'haṃ viśeṣataḥ
bhūteśaṃ giriśaṃ sthāṇuṃ devadevaṃ triśūlinam

134. bhavanto 'pi hi taṃ devaṃ śaṃbhuṃ govṛṣavāhanam
prapadyadhvaṃ sapatnīkāḥ saputrāḥ śaraṇaṃ śivam

135. vartadhvaṃ tatprasādena karmayogena śaṅkaram
pūjayadhvaṃ mahādevaṃ gopatiṃ bhūtibhūṣaṇam

136. evam ukte 'tha munayaḥ śaunakādyā maheśvaram
praṇemuḥ śāśvataṃ sthāṇuṃ vyāsaṃ satyavatīsutam

137. abruvan hṛṣṭamanasaḥ kṛṣṇadvaipāyanaṃ prabhum
sākṣād eva hṛṣīkeśaṃ sarvalokamaheśvaram

138. bhavatprasādād acalā śaraṇye govṛṣadhvaje
idānīṃ jāyate bhaktir yā devair api durlabhā

139. kathayasva muniśreṣṭha karmayogam anuttamam
yenāsau bhagavān īśaḥ samārādhyo mumukṣubhiḥ

140. tvatsaṃnidhāv eṣa sūtaḥ śṛṇotu bhagavadvacaḥ
tadvad ākhilalokānāṃ rakṣaṇaṃ dharmasaṃgraham

141. yaduktaṃ devadevena viṣṇunā kūrmarūpiṇā
pṛṣṭena munibhiḥ pūrvaṃ śakreṇāmṛtamanthane

142. śrutvā satyavatīsūnuḥ karmayogaṃ sanātanam
munīnāṃ bhāṣitaṃ kṛṣṇaḥ provāca susamāhitaḥ

143. ya imaṃ paṭhate nityaṃ saṃvādaṃ kṛttivāsasaḥ
sanatkumārapramukhaiḥ sarvapāpaiḥ pramucyate

144. śrāvayed vā dvijān śuddhān brahmacaryaparāyaṇān
yo vā vicārayed arthaṃ sa yāti paramāṃ gatim

145. yaś caitac chṛṇuyān nityaṃ bhaktiyukto dṛḍhavrataḥ
sarvapāpavinirmukto brahmaloke mahīyate

146. tasmāt sarvaprayatnena paṭhitavyo manīṣibhiḥ
śrotavyaś cātha mantavyo viśeṣād brāhmaṇaiḥ sadā

Endnotes

1. *dharmatatparaiḥ* is a correction of the critical edition's *dharmatparaiḥ.*

2. Using the variant reading *aśeṣasaṃsāraduḥkhanāśanam uttamam* instead of the critical edition's *aśeṣasaṃsāraduḥkhanāśam anuttamam.*

3. *pradakṣiṇīkṛtya* is a correction of the critical edition's *dakṣiṇīkṛtya.*

4. *tapo ghoraṃ* is a correction of the critical edition's *tapoghoraṃ.*

5. *kiṃkāraṇam* is a correction of the critical edition's *kiṃ kāraṇam.*

6. *bhagavadvākyaṃ* is a correction of the critical edition's *bhagavad vākyaṃ.*

7. Using the variant reading *yaṃ . . . svātmany ātmānam īśvaram ananyatejasaṃ* instead of the critical edition's *yaḥ . . . svātmanyā yogam īśvaram ananyatejase.*

8. *savāsudevam* is a correction of the critical edition's *sa vāsudevam.*

9. Using the variant reading *baddhāḥ* instead of the critical edition's *baddhaḥ.*

10. Using the variant reading *anyathājñānāt tattvaṃ* instead of the critical edition's *anyathā jñānaṃ tac ca.*

11. *na tv* is a correction of the critical edition's *natv.*

12. Using the variant reading *māyāmayaṃ* instead of the critical edition's *māyāmayo.*

13. *samāhitā* is a correction of the critical edition's *samahitā.*

14. Using the variant reading *kālāgnir* instead of the critical edition's *kālo 'gnir.*

15. Using the variant reading *niyataṃ* instead of the critical edition's *niyataḥ.*

16. *parā śaktir* is a correction of the critical edition's *parāśaktir.*

17. *yatpādapaṅkajaṃ* is a correction of the critical edition's *yat pādapaṅkajaṃ*

18. Using the variant reading *paraṃ ca* instead of the critical edition's *tatparaṃ ca.*

19. Using the variant reading *brahmā viṣṇuḥ* instead of the critical edition's *brahmāviśvaṃ.*

20. *smaḥ* is a correction of the critical edition's *sma.*

21. *prāha* is a correction of the critical edition's *prāhaḥ.*

22. Using the variant reading *prabhavo 'vyayaḥ* instead of the critical edition's *prabhavāvyayaḥ.*

23. Using the variant reading *svayambhūvidhicoditaḥ* instead of the critical edition's *svayaṃbhūr vidhicoditaḥ.*

24. *māyā nimittam* is a correction of the critical edition's *māyānimittam;* using the variant reading *upāśritā* instead of the critical edition's *apāśritā.*

25. *anantāḥ* is a correction of the critical edition's *anantā*.

26. Using the variant reading *anādimadhyanidhanaṃ* instead of the critical edition's *anādimadhyaṃ tiṣṭhantaṃ*.

27. Using the variant reading *param avyaktaṃ* instead of the critical edition's *paramaṃ vyaktaṃ*.

28. *bibheti* is a correction of the critical edition's *vibheti*.

29. *yuñjantīha* is a correction of the critical edition's *yuñjatīha*.

30. Although not listed in the apparatus of the critical edition, I suggest that *pārameśvaraḥ,* not *parameśvaraḥ,* is a likely reading of this verse.

31. *ekacittatā yogo* is a correction of the critical edition's *ekacittatāyogo*.

32. *manaḥśuddhir* is a correction of the critical edition's *manaḥ śuddhir*.

33. *jyotiḥsvarūpiṇam* is a correction of the critical edition's *jyotiḥ svarūpiṇam*.

34. *arpitamanobuddhir* is a correction of the critical edition's *arpitamano buddhir*.

35. Using the variant reading *yogīśo* instead of the critical edition's *yogīśaṃ*.

36. Using the variant reading *dadāmi* instead of the critical edition's *dadāti*.

37. *labdhavān* is a correction of the critical edition's *labdhavād*.

List of Concordances

What follows is a list of passages in the Īśvara Gītā that are identical or nearly identical to passages from the Bhagavad Gītā, Kaṭha Upaniṣad, Śvetāśvatara Upaniṣad, or Taittirīya Upaniṣad. The letters "a," "b," "c," and "d" are used to signify the first, second, third, and fourth quarters of each verse, respectively. For instance, BhG. 5.15cd means the third and fourth quarters of chapter 5, verse 15, of the Bhagavad Gītā. "=" means "identical to;" "cf." notes similarity between verse quarters.

This list is based on the list of concordances in P.-E. Dumont's 1934 publication, *L'Īśvaragītā: Le Chant de Śiva*. It is, however, updated to correspond to the critical editions of each of the relevant texts. It is also expanded to note additional similarities between passages that Dumont does not list, including passages from the Taittirīya Upaniṣad. For a discussion of the significance of some of the apparent borrowings in the Īśvara Gītā, please refer to the introduction.

BhG. = Bhagavad Gītā
Kaṭh. = Kaṭha Upaniṣad
Śvet. = Śvetāśvatara Upaniṣad
Tait. = Taittirīya Upaniṣad

2.33a	= Kaṭh. 6.14a
2.33b	cf. Kaṭh. 6.14b
2.34	= BhG. 13.30
2.38cd	cf. BhG. 5.15cd
2.42c	= BhG. 5.5c
2.42d	cf. BhG. 5.5d
2.47ab	cf. Śvet. 3.19ab
2.48	cf. BhG. 7.26

3.2	= BhG. 13.13; Śvet. 3.16
3.3ab	= BhG. 13.14ab; Śvet. 3.17ab
3.7a	cf. BhG. 9.4a
3.7bc	= BhG. 9.4bc
3.11ab	cf. BhG. 13.21ab
3.18ab	cf. Kaṭh. 6.7a
3.18d	cf. Kaṭh. 3.10d
3.19ab	= Kaṭh. 3.11ab
3.19b	cf. Kaṭh. 6.8a
4.12d	= BhG. 9.31d
4.14a	= BhG. 9.26a
4.15	cf. Śvet. 6.18
5.24c	= Śvet. 3.20a
5.27a	cf. Śvet. 6.1d
5.35a	= BhG. 11.18a
5.35b	= BhG. 11.18b; BhG. 11.38b
5.35c	= BhG. 11.18c
5.35d	cf. BhG. 11.18d
5.37b	= BhG. 8.9d
6.46ab	= BhG. 7.4ab
7.4c	= BhG. 10.21a
7.5c	cf. BhG. 10.27c
7.5d	= BhG. 10.31b
7.7a	cf. BhG. 10.37c
7.7d	= BhG. 10.26d
7.12c	cf. BhG. 10.22a
7.16b	= BhG. 10.30b
8.3a	= BhG. 14.3a
8.3b	cf. BhG. 14.3b
8.7	cf. BhG. 14.4
8.10d	= BhG. 5.5d
8.10	= BhG. 13.27
8.11	= BhG. 13.28
8.17c	= Śvet. 3.20a
9.10d	= Kaṭh. 3.9d
9.11a	cf. BhG. 7.7c
9.12abc	= Tait. 2.4.1abc

9.12d	cf. Tait. 2.4.1d
9.13ab	= Śvet. 3.8ab
9.15b	cf. Śvet. 6.6d
9.18ab	= Śvet. 6.11ab
9.18c	cf. Śvet. 6.12c
9.18d	= Kaṭh. 5.13d; cf. Śvet. 6.12d
9.19abc	= Śvet. 3.11abc
11.71ab	= BhG. 4.10ab
11.71cd	cf. BhG. 4.10cd
11.72ab	= BhG. 4.11ab
11.74a	cf. BhG. 18.57ab
11.75ab	= BhG. 12.13ab
11.75c	cf. BhG. 12.13c
11.75d	= BhG. 12.14d; BhG. 12.16d
11.76	= BhG. 12.14
11.77abc	= BhG. 12.15abc
11.77d	cf. BhG. 12.15d
11.78abc	= BhG. 12.16abc
11.78c	= BhG. 14.25c
11.78d	= BhG. 12.17d
11.79abc	= BhG. 12.19abc
11.81ab	= BhG. 18.57ab
11.81c	= BhG. 3.30c
11.82ab	= BhG. 4.20ab
11.82cd	cf. BhG. 4.20cd
11.82d	cf. BhG. 4.22d
11.83abc	= BhG. 4.21abc
11.83d	cf. BhG. 4.21d
11.84ab	cf. BhG. 4.22ab
11.86bc	= BhG. 10.9bc
11.87c	cf. BhG. 10.11c
11.87d	= BhG. 10.11d
11.88cd	= BhG. 9.22cd
11.89b	cf. BhG. 9.23a
11.90ab	cf. BhG. 9.23ab
11.104b	cf. BhG. 9.32b
11.117bc	cf. BhG. 5.18bc
11.143d	= BhG. 10.3d

Glossary of Sanskrit Names and Terms

Adharma: "Anti-*dharma*," that which is contrary to sacred law. Adharma is apotheosized as the god of immorality (also see entry for Dharma).

Āditya: "The son of Aditi," an epithet that may refer to any one of a group of solar deities, especially Sūrya, god of the sun.

Agni: Fire, also deified as the god of fire.

Airāvata: Indra's elephant, considered the greatest of all elephants.

Aṅgiras: A sage and teacher. He is a son of Brahmā and is associated with the planet Jupiter.

Arjuna: The warrior who received teachings from the god Kṛṣṇa in the Bhagavad Gītā.

Aśvin: "Possessed of horses," the name of twin gods who appear in the sky before dawn in a golden chariot drawn by horses. They are the physicians among the gods.

Atri: A great sage, one of the mind-born sons of Brahmā who is included among the *saptarṣi* (seven sages).

Badarikā: A holy place in the Himālaya mountains and the site of the hermitage where the Īśvara Gītā's teaching takes place. It is associated with Śiva and with Viṣṇu in his dual form as Nara-Nārāyaṇa.

Balarāma: The older brother of Kṛṣṇa.

Bharadvāja: A great sage descended from Aṅgiras, often considered one of the *saptarṣi* (seven sages).

Bhava: "Existence," a name for a peaceful form of Śiva. In the Īśvara Gītā, it is this form to which Śiva reverts after he reveals his awe-inspiring form as lord of the dance.

Bhṛgu: A great sage. In Vedic mythology, he is a son of Varuṇa. In post-Vedic mythology, he is considered one of the sons of Brahmā.

Brahmā: The creator god, often portrayed as one of the trio of gods responsible for the creation, preservation, and destruction of the universe.

Brahman: The ultimate reality and cause of the universe according to Vedānta philosophers. Some philosophers depict Brahman as an abstract impersonal reality beyond any god; others say that Brahman is another name for god.

Brahmin: A member of the highest of the four classes (*varṇas*), the priestly class.

Cāraṇa: A type of demigod associated with singing and music.

Dakṣa: "Skillful," one of the Ādityas and a son of Brahmā. He is remembered in the Purāṇas as the father of Śiva's consort Satī.

Devakī: The mother of Kṛṣṇa and Balarāma.

Dharma: In most Hindu contexts, *dharma* refers to the sacred law that faithful worshippers are expected to follow. *Dharma* is context-specific, and varies depending on factors such as class (*varṇa*), gender, and stage of life (*āśrama*). Dharma is apotheosized in mythology as the god of sacred law.

Gandharva: A type of male celestial being, often considered a celestial musician or attendant of the gods.

Gaṇeśa: The elephant-headed god who is son of Śiva and Pārvatī. He is widely worshipped as the "remover of obstacles."

Garuḍa: The name of a mythical bird, considered to be the vehicle of Viṣṇu.

Gotama: A sage, often considered one of the *saptarṣi* (seven sages). He is descended from the sage Aṅgiras. He should not be confused with Siddhārtha Gautama, the Buddha.

Guṇa: In Sāṃkhya philosophy, there are three *guṇas*, colored white, red, and black, that can be translated as purity (*sattva*), agitation (*rajas*), and inertia (*tamas*). These three *guṇas* constitute the material world (*prakṛti* and its twenty-three evolutes), and all aspects of the material world can be understood as being an admixture of these three *guṇas* in different proportions.

Hara: "Seizer," a name of the god Śiva.

Hari: "Yellow," a name of the god Viṣṇu.

Hiraṇyagarbha: "Golden-womb," a name of the creator god. He is described in the Īśvara Gītā as being born from Śiva's body in order to create the world.

Indra: The king of the gods. Indra wields a thunderbolt and rides the elephant Airāvata. Although one of the most important gods of Vedic mythology, by the time of the Īśvara Gītā he was considered inferior to Śiva and Viṣṇu.

Īśāna: "Ruler," an epithet of Śiva. This name is also applied to one of the Rudras.

Jaigīṣavya: The name of a great sage and yogi.

Jyeṣṭhasāma: A particular chant from the Sāma Veda.

Kaṇāda: A sage and founder of the Vaiśeṣika system of philosophy.

Kapila: A sage and founder of the Sāṃkhya system of philosophy. In the Purāṇas, he is often considered to be an incarnation of Viṣṇu.

Kṛṣṇa: "Dark," the god who narrated the teachings of the Bhagavad Gītā to the warrior Arjuna, and is also featured in many Purāṇas. Many Hindus consider Kṛṣṇa to be an incarnation of the god Viṣṇu.

Kṛṣṇa Dvaipāyana: "Island-born Kṛṣṇa," an epithet of the sage Vyāsa.

Kubera: The god of wealth.

Manu: The mythical first man and author of several texts. In the plural, "the Manus" also refer to the first beings created by god at the beginning of each "age of Manu" (*manvantara*).

Marīci: "Ray of light," the name of a sage.

Marut: Generic name for the storm gods who bear golden weapons and are allied with Indra.

Meru: The name of a mythical golden mountain, the center of the world according to Purāṇic cosmologies.

Nara: The name of a sage or god, sometimes considered to be a twin incarnation of Viṣṇu along with Nārāyaṇa. In the Nara-Nārāyaṇa pairing, Nara is identified with Arjuna and Nārāyaṇa with Kṛṣṇa.

Nārāyaṇa: The name of a sage or god, sometimes considered to be a twin incarnation of Viṣṇu along with Nara. In the Īśvara Gītā, this is the most common name for the god Viṣṇu.

Nirṛti: "Destruction," usually given divine form as the goddess of death, daughter of Adharma ("immorality") and Hiṃsā ("violence"). The Īśvara Gītā describes Nirṛti as male rather than female.

Nirvāṇa: "Extinguishing," a term used especially among Buddhists to denote the cessation of suffering and the freedom from the cycle of birth and death. It is also used in Hindu texts, often as a synonym for *mokṣa*, "liberation."

Pañcaśikha: "Five tufted," the name of a teacher of Sāṃkhya philosophy.

Parāśara: A sage, grandson of Vasiṣṭha and father of Vyāsa.

Pārvatī: "Daughter of Parvata," a goddess, daughter of the Himālaya mountains and consort of Śiva.

Pināka: The name of Śiva's bow.

Prahlāda: "Joyful," the name of a demon (*asura*) prince, son of Hiraṇyakaśipu, who worshipped Viṣṇu devoutly and opposed his own father.

Pulaha: A sage, one of the sons of Brahmā.

Purāṇa: "Ancient," the name of a genre of texts composed primarily in the medieval period. The major Sanskrit Purāṇas are traditionally counted as eighteen, divided into three groups of six. Six of these texts are devoted to the god Brahmā, six to Viṣṇu, and six to Śiva. The Īśvara Gītā itself makes up a small part of the Kūrma Purāṇa, the Purāṇa that takes its name from the tortoise (*kūrma*) form of Viṣṇu.

Puṣkara: "Blue lotus," the name of one of the seven major continents according to the cosmology of the Purāṇas.

Rāma: A hero and the protagonist of the epic poem Rāmāyaṇa, usually considered one of the incarnations of the god Viṣṇu.

Ṛkṣa: A name for any of the seven stars of the Ursa Major constellation, associated with the seven sages (*ṛṣis*). Although accounts vary, one list from the Bṛhadāraṇyaka Upaniṣad includes Gotama, Bharadvāja, Viśvāmitra, Jamadagni, Vasiṣṭha, Kaśyapa, and Atri (Bṛhadāraṇyaka Upaniṣad 2.2.4).

Rudra: "Roarer," a dangerous Vedic god. In post-Vedic mythology, Rudra is another name for Śiva. The Īśvara Gītā describes Rudra as the aspect of Śiva that causes the world's destruction, along with his other aspects Brahmā (the creator) and Nārāyaṇa (the preserver). In the plural, "the Rudras" are a group of eleven storm gods closely associated with Rudra-Śiva. In the Īśvara Gītā, one of the sages in the audience listening to Śiva's teachings is also named Rudra.

Sādhya: The name of a class of demigods.

Śakra: "Powerful," an epithet of Indra, king of the gods.

Śakti: "Power," often apotheosized as a feminine force or a goddess. In the Īśvara Gītā, Lord Śiva possesses powers such as *māyā*, the power to create worldly forms. The gods Brahmā, Nārāyaṇa, and Rudra are also described as Śiva's powers for the world's creation, preservation, and destruction, respectively.

Sāma: The Sāma Veda, one of the four Vedas, contains sacred songs (*sāmans*) designed to be chanted during sacrifice.

Śambhu: "Granting happiness," a name for Śiva in his benevolent form.

Sāṃkhya: A school of philosophy that teaches of the existence of two basic realities, spirit (*puruṣa*) and matter (*prakṛti*). Matter is a dynamic feminine principle that evolves into twenty-three more principles (*tattvas*) for a total of twenty-five principles in all. Although some Sāṃkhya texts claim that matter is eternal and without any higher cause, theistic texts like the Īśvara Gītā understand god to be the ultimate cause of spirit and matter. In the Īśvara Gītā, the word *sāṃkhya* is also used to refer to the path of knowledge generally (as opposed to *yoga*, the path of practical discipline). For a summary of the tenets of the Sāṃkhya philosophical school, see King (1999:166–89).

Saṃvarta: A sage descended from Aṅgiras.

Sanaka: "Ancient," a sage, one of the mind-born sons of Brahmā. He is the brother of Sanandana, Sanātana, and Sanatkumāra.

Sanandana: "Joyful," a sage, one of the mind-born sons of Brahmā. He is the brother of Sanaka, Sanātana, and Sanatkumāra.

Sanātana: "Eternal," a sage, one of the mind-born sons of Brahmā. He is the brother of Sanaka, Sanandana, and Sanatkumāra.

Sanatkumāra: "Eternal youth," a sage, one of the mind-born sons of Brahmā. He is the brother of Sanaka, Sanandana, and Sanātana.

Śaṅkara: "Auspicious," an epithet of Śiva. He is also depicted as one of the eleven Rudras, forms of Śiva. In modern usage, "Śaṅkara" is often used to refer to the philosopher Ādi Śaṅkarācārya, founder of the Advaita Vedānta school.

Saptarṣi: "Seven sages," a group of sages that is also said to correspond to the names of the stars in the Ursa Major constellation according to Indian astrology. Although accounts vary, one list from the Bṛhadāraṇyaka Upaniṣad includes Gotama, Bharadvāja, Viśvāmitra, Jamadagni, Vasiṣṭha, Kaśyapa, and Atri (Bṛhadāraṇyaka Upaniṣad 2.2.4).

Sarasvatī: The goddess of poetry, learning, and music. She is the consort of the god Brahmā.

Śatarudrīya: A hymn in the Yajur Veda praising the hundred forms of the god Rudra.

Satī: "Good woman," a form of the goddess who is the consort of Śiva. In the Purāṇas she is depicted as a daughter of Dakṣa. She immolated herself in protest after her father refused to invite her husband to a Vedic sacrifice.

Satyavatī: "Truthful," the mother of Vyāsa. According to legend, she was the daughter of a fisherman who begat Vyāsa with the sage Parāśara. She later married King Śantanu.

Satyavrata: "Truthful vow," the name of a royal sage.

Śaunaka: The name of a great sage.

Sāvitrī: the name of a famous mantra from the Ṛg Veda that is also known as Gāyatrī. Sāvitrī is also deified in mythology as the wife of the god Brahmā and the mother of the four Vedas.

Śeṣa: "Remainder," the name of a mythical thousand-headed serpent whom the god Viṣṇu rests upon between world-cycles.

Siddha: "Accomplished," an epithet used for certain extraordinary yogis who have attained supernormal powers known as *siddhis*. Siddhas are sometimes considered demigods, or even to have conquered death itself.

Śiva: "Auspicious," the name of one of the major gods of classical Hinduism. Although sometimes considered the god of destruction, the Īśvara Gītā portrays him as the absolute creator, preserver, and destroyer of the entire world. He is known by many other epithets, such as Īśvara ("the lord").

Skanda: "Attacker," a war god and son of Śiva.

Soma: A drink that was worshipped as a god and used by priests during Vedic sacrifice. In post-Vedic texts such as the Purāṇas, it is also the god associated with the moon.

Śrī: The goddess of wealth, also known as Lakṣmī. She is the consort of Viṣṇu.

Śukra: "Bright," a sage who was the son of Bhṛgu. He is associated with the planet Venus.

Sūrya: The sun, which is also deified as the god of the sun.

Sūta: Whereas the word *sūta* can sometimes just be translated "bard," the name Sūta in this text refers to the bard Lomaharṣaṇa, student of the sage Vyāsa and reciter of many Purāṇas.

Svastika: Meaning "auspicious," this word often refers to a religious symbol in the shape of a cross with bent arms. In the Īśvara Gītā and other works on yoga, it also refers to a sitting posture (*āsana*) in which the right foot is tucked between the left calf and left thigh.

Umā: a goddess, daughter of the Himālaya mountains and consort of Śiva. She is also known as Pārvatī.

Upaniṣad: The Upaniṣads are the part of the Vedas that contain teachings of the true nature of the self (*ātman*) and its relationship with *brahman*, the ultimate reality. These are the texts that are analyzed by the sub-schools of Vedānta philosophy.

Vaiśeṣika: The name of a school of philosophy reputedly founded by the sage Kaṇāda. It teaches that the universe came into being through the agglomeration of atomic particles.

Vālmīki: The sage considered by tradition to have authored the epic poem Rāmāyaṇa, "The Deeds of Rāma."

Vāmadeva: This epithet may refer either to a great sage or to one of the Rudras, the eleven storm gods often seen as aspects of Śiva.

Vārāṇasī: A city often considered the holiest by worshippers of Śiva. It is located on the banks of the Ganges River in northeastern India. It is also known by the names Banāras and Kāśī.

Varuṇa: A major Vedic god responsible for upholding order on heaven and earth. In post-Vedic mythology he is considered god of the oceans and rivers.

Vasu: "Wealthy," a class of gods of the atmosphere.

Vāsudeva: "Son of Vasudeva," a patronymic name given to Viṣṇu or Kṛṣṇa.

Vasiṣṭha: "Wealthiest," the name of a great sage, often considered one of the *saptarṣi* (seven sages).

Vedānta: "End of the Vedas," originally a name for the Upaniṣads, the part of the Vedas most concerned with philosophical speculation. In later times, Vedānta came to refer to a tradition of philosophy and exegesis based on the Upaniṣads. The Vedānta philosophical school's main concern is to analyze the nature of the ultimate reality (*brahman*) and its relation to the self (*ātman*).

Vedas: The most authoritative texts for most Hindu traditions. There are four Vedas: Ṛg, Yajur, Sāma, and Atharva.

Vīrabhadra: A terrifying form of the god Śiva created from his own body to destroy Dakṣa's sacrifice after Śiva was dishonored by Dakṣa.

Vīraka: "Little hero," another name for Nandin, one of the most important leaders of Śiva's troops (*gaṇas*). This Nandin should not be confused with Śiva's bull, who was also called Nandin in later times.

Viṣṇu: The preserver god, one of the most important of gods worshipped in classical Hinduism. He is usually considered to have many incarnations (*avataras*), including the heroes Rāma and Kṛṣṇa. In the Īśvara Gītā he is often called Nārāyaṇa.

Viśvakarman: "All-maker," the craftsman and architect among the gods.

Vyāsa: A scholar who, according to Hindu traditions, authored the Mahābhārata and the Purāṇas, as well as a commentary on Patañjali's Yoga Sūtras. He is considered the author of the Īśvara Gītā, as this text is part of the Kūrma Purāṇa.

Yajur Veda: One of the four Vedas. The Yajur Veda is a manual of directions for the performance of Vedic sacrifice, including formulations of mantras.

Yoga: In the Īśvara Gītā, *yoga* often denotes "practical discipline," such as techniques of mental concentration, as opposed to philosophical speculation (e.g., verses 2.40, 2.41). It can also mean "method" or "way" (as at 11.72). Etymologically, the word *yoga* means "union" or "yoking." According to the Īśvara Gītā, the highest *yoga* is the yogi's yoking himself to Lord Śiva. In this text it does not usually signify a specific school of philosophy, nor does it refer primarily to athletic postures such as headstands and shoulder stands. For more on the meanings of *yoga,* refer to the introduction.

Yogi: A practitioner of yoga. In the Īśvara Gītā, Śiva is depicted as the greatest of yogis, and instructs his audience of sages in the practice of yoga.

Bibliography

Bisschop, Peter C. (2006). *Early Śaivism and the Skandapurāṇa: Sects and Centres.* Groningen: Egbart Forsten.

Brown, C. Mackenzie (ed. and tr.) (1998). *The Devi Gita: The Song of the Goddess*. Albany: State University of New York Press.

Bryant, Edwin F. (ed. and tr.) (2009). *The Yoga Sūtras of Patañjali.* New York: North Point Press.

Cush, Denise (ed.) (2007). *Encyclopedia of Hinduism*. London: Routledge.

Chakraborti, Haripada (ed. and tr.) (1970). *Pāśupata Sūtram with Pañcārtha-Bhāṣya of Kauṇḍinya*. Calcutta: Academic Publishers.

Dasgupta, Surendranath (1975). *A History of Indian Philosophy, Volume V.* Delhi: Motilal Banarsidass.

Dimmitt, Cornelia and J.A.B. van Buitenen (1978). *Classical Hindu Mythology: A Reader in the Sanskrit Purāṇas*. Philadelphia: Temple University Press.

Doniger, Wendy (ed.) (1993). *Purāṇa Perennis: Reciprocity and Transformation in Hindu and Jaina Texts*. Albany: State University of New York Press.

Dumont, P.-E. (1934). *L'Īśvaragītā: Le Chant de Śiva*. Baltimore: Johns Hopkins Press.

Dyczkowski, Mark S.G. (1988). *The Canon of the Saivagama and the Kubjika Tantras of the Western Kaula Tradition.* Albany: State University of New York Press.

Edgerton, Franklin (1934). "Review of *L'Īśvaragītā: Le Chant de Śiva* by P.-E. Dumont," *Journal of the American Oriental Society* 54(3):306–10.

Flood, Gavin (1996). *An Introduction to Hinduism.* Cambridge: Cambridge University Press.

——— (ed.) (2003). *The Blackwell Companion to Hinduism*. Maldon, MA: Blackwell Publishing.

Gambhirananda, Swami (2006). *Bhagavad Gītā with the Commentary of Śaṅkarācārya.* Kolkata: Advaita Ashrama.

Gandhi, M. K. (1965). *Gita—My Mother*. Bombay: Bharatiya Vidya Bhavan.

Goldberg, Ellen (2002). *The Lord Who Is Half Woman: Ardhanarīśvara in Indian and Feminist Perspective.* Albany: State University of New York Press.

Goldman, Robert and Sally Sutherland (1999). *Devavāṇīpraveśikā: An Introduction to the Sanskrit Language*. Berkeley: Center for South Asia Studies.

Goudriaan, Teun (1978). *Māyā Divine and Human*. Delhi: Motilal Banarsidass.

Gonda, Jan (1979). "The Śatarudrīya," in M. Nagatomi, B. K. Matilal and J. M. Masson (eds.), *Sanskrit and Indian Studies: Essays in Honour of Daniel H. H. Ingalls*. Dordrecht: Reidel, pp. 75–91.

Gupta, Anand Swarup (ed.) (1971). *The Kūrma Purāṇa*. Varanasi: All-India Kashiraj Trust.

Hadot, Pierre (2002). *What is Ancient Philosophy*? Cambridge: Harvard University Press.

Halbfass, Wilhelm (1990). *Tradition and Reflection: Explorations in Indian Thought*. Albany: State University of New York Press.

Hara, Minoru (2002). *Pāśupata Studies*. Vienna: Sammlung de Nobili.

Hazra, R.C. (1987)[1940]. *Studies in the Purāṇic Records on Hindu Rites and Customs*. Delhi: Motilal Banarsidass.

Hulin, Michel (1993). "Doctrines et comportements 'cyniques' dans certaines sects hindoues anciennes et contemporaines," in Goulet-Caze, M.-O. and R. Goulet (eds.), *Le Cynisme ancien et ses prolongements*. Paris: Presses universitaires de France, pp. 557–70.

Ingalls, Daniel (1962). "Cynics and Pāśupatas: The Seeking of Dishonor." *Harvard Theological Review* 55(4):281–98.

King, Richard (1999). *Indian Philosophy: An Introduction to Hindu and Buddhist Thought*. Washington, DC: Georgetown University Press.

Larson, Gerald and Ram Shankar Bhattacharya (eds.) (1987). *Encyclopedia of Indian Philosophies vol. IV, Sāṃkhya: A Dualist Tradition in Indian Philosophy*. Princeton: Princeton University Press.

Malinar, Angelika (2009). *Bhagavadgītā: Doctrines and Contexts*. New York: Oxford University Press.

Miller, Barbara Stoler (1986). *The Bhagavad-Gita: Krishna's Counsel in Time of War*. New York: Columbia University Press.

Minor, Robert (ed.) (1986). *Modern Indian Interpreters of the Bhagavad Gita*. Albany: State University of New York Press.

Nicholson, Andrew J. (2010). *Unifying Hinduism: Philosophy and Identity in Indian Intellectual History*. New York: Columbia University Press.

Nilakantan, Ratnam. (1989). *Gītās in the Mahābhārata and the Purāṇas*. Delhi: Nag Publishers.

Olivelle, Patrick (ed. and tr.) (1992). *Saṃnyāsa Upaniṣads: Hindu Scriptures on Asceticism and Renunciation*. New York: Oxford University Press.

——— (ed. and tr.) (1996). *Upaniṣads*. New York: Oxford University Press.

——— (ed. and tr.) (2005). *Manu's Code of Law: A Critical Edition and Translation of the Mānava-Dharmaśāstra*. New York: Oxford University Press.

Piantelli, Mario (ed. and tr.) (1980). *Īśvaragītā, o, Poema del Signore*. Parma: L. Battei.

Pintchman, Tracy (1994). *The Rise of the Goddess in the Hindu Tradition*. Albany: State University of New York Press.

Raghavan, V. (1952). *Yantras or Mechanical Contrivances in Ancient India*. Bangalore: Indian Institute of Culture.

Rocher, Ludo (1986). *The Purāṇas*. History of Indian Literature, v. 2, fasc. 3. Wiesbaden: O. Harrassowitz.

Sanderson, Alexis (1988). "Saivism and the Tantric Traditions," in Stewart Sutherland (ed.), *The World's Religions*, pp. 660–704. London: Routledge.

———. (2005). "The Lākulas: New Evidence of a System Intermediate between Pañcārthika Pāśupatism and Āgamic Śaivism," *Indian Philosophical Annual* 24: 143–217.

Sastri, R. Anantakrishna (ed.) (1940). *The Pāśupata Sūtras with Pañcārthabhāṣya of Kauṇḍinya* (Trivandrum Sanskrit Series no. 143). Trivandrum: Oriental Manuscripts Library of the University of Travancore.

Smith, Travis L. (2008). *The Sacred Center and its Peripheries: Śaivism and the Vārāṇasī Sthala-Purāṇas*. PhD diss., Columbia University.

Tarkaratna, Ramamaya (ed.) (1990). *The Atharvana Upanishads* (Bibliotheca Indica v. 76). Osnabrück: Biblio Verlag.

Upadhyaya, Ganga Prasad (tr.) (2008). *The Light of Truth: English Translation of Svami Dayanand's Sathyartha Prakasha*. Delhi: Govindram Hasanand.

White, David Gordon (2009). *Sinister Yogis*. Chicago: University of Chicago Press.

———. (2012). *Yoga in Practice*. Princeton: Princeton University Press.